TEACHING
IN THE
Online Classroom

TEACHING
IN THE
Online Classroom

Surviving and Thriving in the New Normal

Doug Lemov and the Teach Like a Champion Team

JB JOSSEY-BASS™
A Wiley Brand

Jossey-Bass
A Wiley Imprint
111 River St, Hoboken, NJ 07030
www.josseybass.com

Jossey-Bass books and products are available through most bookstores. To contact Jossey-Bass directly, call our Customer Care Department within the U.S. at 800–956–7739, outside the U.S. at +1 317 572 3986, or fax +1 317 572 4002.

Wiley also publishes its books in a variety of electronic formats and by print-on-demand. Some material included with standard print versions of this book may not be included in e-books or in print-on-demand. If this book refers to media such as a CD or DVD that is not included in the version you purchased, you may download this material at http://booksupport.wiley.com. For more information about Wiley products, visit www.wiley.com.

Library of Congress Cataloging-in-Publication Data is Available:

ISBNs: 9781119762935 (paperback), 9781119762881 (ePub), 9781119762959 (ePDF)

Cover Design: Paul Mccarthy
Cover Art: © Vasilkovs/Shutterstock.com

Printed in the United States of America

FIRST EDITION

SKY10026953_051121

Contents

Introduction

Remote Teaching and the New Normal
Doug Lemov and Erica Woolway

There are a few tiny, beautiful moments in one of Eric Snider's remote English lessons with his students at Achievement First Iluminar Mayoral Academy Middle School in Cranston, Rhode Island. The class is reading Rita Williams-Garcia's *One Crazy Summer*, and Eric asks if anyone is willing to try to answer a question that they know is difficult. Eric has already told them, calmly and without judgment, that many of them misunderstood a key passage—that the question they've been asked to answer is a hard one. Many of the students are undaunted, and they volunteer. "Thanks, James. Thanks, George. Thanks, Jaylee," he says as each hand is raised. He's showing students that he sees them embrace the challenge. Soon, there are more volunteers. "Wow, ton of hands here. I appreciate it."

It's a great moment, because it reminds us how important it is for people to feel seen. Telling someone how much you appreciate what they do in the face of challenges can help bring out their best, online as much as in person.

This moment also reminds us that the act of observing others can influence people's behavior. We become—or can become—more like what we choose to observe. "The human body has about 11M sensory receptors," James Clear writes in *Atomic Habits*. "Approximately 10M of those are dedicated to sight . . . a small change in what you see can lead to a big shift in what you do." Good models are powerful.

The clip ends, as you will later see, with a student answering the difficult question beautifully and compellingly, from the back seat of her family's car. It's a difficult world right now, but she's managed to adapt, and she's brought her A game.

Teachers, too, have been asked to do what they know is difficult: to shift, without warning, to an unfamiliar universe—one where we interact with our students remotely, as if through a tiny keyhole in the classroom door. Each of the young people we care about now appears as a small image in the corner of our computer screen (sometimes not even that).

Nearly everything about teaching has changed for teachers over the past few months except the fact that students need us. And so it's incumbent upon us a profession to learn new methods to reach them as quickly and effectively as possible.

This book is about applying the lessons of that moment from Eric's classroom to teachers. In it we'll show you, with appreciation, tiny moments from the classes of real teachers working online. We'll share insights and discuss principles from those examples to help you adapt as successfully as possible to our "New Normal" of remote teaching or some combination of remote and classroom education. And in doing so we hope to show our appreciation for you and for the teachers whose work we share.

No one asked for the world to change this way, but it has. As teachers, that means there's work to be done. If you're reading this, you realize and embrace that fact. We're grateful to you, and our goal is to pay you back for that commitment. And the good news is that it's not just that teachers have jumped in, in the face of difficulty, and done the work. It's that they have done the work and begun to find solutions to the difficult day-to-day challenges of remote teaching. Whenever difficulty presents itself, there is always some teacher, somewhere, who finds a solution.

FACING THE NEW NORMAL, NOW.

In facing new teaching challenges, it's important to remember that while so much of the work has changed (we all now know what Zoom is, for example), much also remains the same. The fundamentals of teaching and the relationships that we know from our previous lives still very much apply. Sometimes we just have to look harder or in different places to see it. As one friend described her life under quarantine, it is a New Normal—totally different but with at least an echo of the familiar.

Since this New Normal began, we've witnessed plenty of challenges in the "classroom"—glitchy internet; good internet but some children lacking a device to access it; students participating from hallways outside their apartments; teachers leading classes with their own children in their laps—but we have seen even more of a can-do attitude, a problem-solving embrace of situations outside our control. There is less looking back over shoulders and more turning to face the future full-on.

It's important to underscore the urgency of this attitude—the absolute necessity of getting better at what we do now, no matter the circumstances.

A recent blog post[1] by Brown University economist Emily Oster used data from her colleague John Freidman's research to show how critical the next months and years of our teaching lives will be. Friedman took data on student progress from the online math platform Zearn, charted it longitudinally, and disaggregated it by income level. Here's the chart:

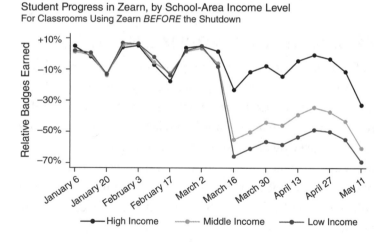

Student Progress in Zearn, by School-Area Income Level
For Classrooms Using Zearn *BEFORE* the Shutdown

The data are based on the rate at which students who were already familiar with online learning progressed through achievement "badges" on Zearn's platform. It's an imperfect measure—on one hand, a lot of the work involves self-study of preproduced materials (asynchronous learning) rather than face-to-face remote interactions with a teacher (synchronous learning); on the other hand, it's data on students who were already doing extensive remote work, and therefore students for whom transitioning online was probably far less of a disruption than it has been for others. Badges may not be a perfect measure of learning, but they offer data that shows us very clearly how being away from classrooms has affected a large group of students in a measurable way—and allowed us to disaggregate that data by income and look for potential disparities and inequities. By those standards, the data are devastating.

"Even for students in the *best-off* districts—the higher-income ones—there is a reduction of about 10% in the badges earned," Oster wrote, "and this seems to get even worse in the most recent weeks. For students in middle- and lower-income school districts, the results are a disaster. There appears to be about a 60% drop in badges earned. That is, kids in these districts are moving through the curriculum at *less than half the pace they did while in school*" (italics in original).

The situation is urgent, but we think the big issues are addressed not insignificantly by our willingness to focus on "small" issues of craft—to improve what we do every day as teachers.

And, at the end of the day, there are some silver linings. A few things will work better online; some students will thrive more there; some things we'll learn will make us better teachers in all settings. There will be some lessons to take back to our old classrooms. We don't mean to ignore that. We just think it's important to be clear that everything we know about teaching suggests that on net the experience online will be less powerful, and what's most worrisome is that it will almost certainly be that way most for the students most at risk already.

It's all hands on deck.

A colleague, a journalist, wrote to us in the midst of the quarantine last April. What did we think was the consensus feeling of teachers? Were they excited? Did they think the future had suddenly arrived as in a day? Or were they more cynical? Were they thinking, *not another damn thing to get trained on*!?

None of the above. We thought a decent summary of the average teacher's opinion was: "This is scary, and I miss the world as it used to be—me, my classroom, my students. But this is reality. The kids need me to be good at this, so I've got to give it my best."

Obviously, no large group of people have opinions that are so easily glossed, but this book is for those teachers who, like us, would not have chosen this course but who, faced with it, are determined to find simple, replicable ways to do it well and serve our students best. In other words, we're no futurists. We won't be making any TED Talks on the seamless, friction-less, automatic teaching future waiting for us if we could just embrace technology.

Like many (most? all?) of you, we hope to be back to classrooms soon. We have spent much of our collective careers studying them—each tiny interaction by each tiny interaction—because we think they matter so much, and because we think that classrooms are uniquely suited to build a culture around students that brings out their best. Classrooms can be a "bright mirror": a place that wraps students in a culture that draws out the best from within them, but also changes them for the better. The ideal learning environment is a classroom where your peers look at you as you share a nascent idea. Their eyes show they value it too. They listen carefully and their words, in response, make the point as well. They help you expand and refine it. Soon it's not really your idea anymore, but the group's collective thinking. Together, you come to a deeper shared understanding.

Humans are finely evolved machines for observing and responding to the other humans around them, having survived as a species by forming social groups. When we are together socially, we can draw on all of the tools that are wired in our brains that make us respond to positive culture. And while an online setting can't provide all the things a classroom can — you can never capture the feeling, for instance, of a room of 30 people hanging on one another's words, somehow actually feeling their responses to a telling insight — the goal must be to get remote learning as close to that as possible. It needs to get across the power of listening and being heard, the way students are drawn in and caused to be engaged, on their toes, and accountable, in the most loving sense of the word, even when they may not feel like it.

On net, we believe, the experience of learning online will likely be less productive for most students than classrooms are. It may be profoundly so for many, and in a way that impacts the most vulnerable learners most. It's a sort of second, educational pandemic, and the best way to fight it, we think, is by focusing on the core of the craft: the foundational moves that shape each interaction with young people and that can improve the experience and mitigate its limitations as much as possible. The word "fundamentals" is important. We seek in online classrooms what we sought in their brick-and-mortar cousins: that which is relatively straightforward to do and easily replicated, and that which can be reused and adapted to make the learning experience richer for students. Those things are most valuable and most worth your time. And as Chip and Dan Heath remind us in one of our favorite books on change management, *Switch*, the size of the solution does not always match the size of the problem. Small changes can have profound effects. We've tried to focus on that here.

Ultimately, we're pragmatists about online learning, informed by a dose of skepticism and a profound belief in people, students, and teachers, all of which may make us useful guides. But even to our most skeptical sides, it's not all bad news. There are a few silver linings, too. We'll find out new things about ourselves and grow our abilities to teach online. We'll discuss some of those in a moment. But first, let us take a step back and tell you more about how we came to write a book about something that, just a few short months ago, was the furthest thing from our mind.

THE CRAFT OF TEACHING

This is a good time to note that we are teachers, too, not just in the sense that we write about and study teaching, but in the sense that we spend most of our time in rooms with groups of people who we are trying to help learn things — in this case the craft of teaching.

We too were caught off guard by the sudden erasure of the classroom. We had a spring full of workshops to design and run and suddenly one day in March they were all cancelled. We wondered, should we close up shop? Hunker down and wait it out? But teaching, and teachers, were in crisis. And in the end we believe that our strength as a group lies in the group itself — our ability to learn together. This is what we'd been doing for ten years: gathering twice a week to watch video of teachers teaching, analyzing their moves and decisions in the tiniest details, and learning as much as we possibly could. If you ask us what we do, we say we study teachers. Could we turn that power on virtual classrooms? After all, one of the few advantages of virtual classrooms is ease of recording. The video had to be out there. Could we watch and study and learn?

Two days after we closed up the office and went home, we gathered—via Zoom—to watch our first batch of video of online teaching. It was from a group of kindergarten and first-grade teachers from a charter school in Brooklyn. Having woken up in a brave new world, there they were, smiling for children who really needed to see them smiling, and giving their best at teaching sight words and story problems from their living rooms and kitchens. They were wonderful, all of them, but one stood out in particular. Her name was Rachel Shin. We all knew at once there was something doubly special there. Her smile and warmth made it feel like she was standing in the room with us. Her lesson was asynchronous—prerecorded for students to watch later—but it was clearly designed to keep students active rather than passive as participants. She told her students to pause the video and complete a problem. She told them to email her another for homework that night. *Dissolve the Screen, Pause Points, Lagging Assessment*: these are all ideas you'll read about later, and each of them emerged, as everything here did, from the study of teachers like Rachel.

We posted a quick article on our blog about what we'd observed. It was the first of many, because after that first day we agreed to put everything on hold, to start watching videos together five days a week, to learn as much as we could as fast as we could and to share it out with teachers as often and directly as we could manage.

At this point, the last thing on our mind was a book. A few weeks later, we tentatively offered a webinar with video study and key teaching principles. It was free, but we limited the size so we could better model the interactivities we were talking about. Registration filled in minutes. This we took as a signal about the scope of the demand, not so much the quality of our supply. Even so, we redoubled our efforts. We just wanted to be able to share things of value and learn more in the process.

At the same time, we had another problem. We realized we would soon have to take everything we did in our training work and move it online. We'd been using Zoom for years to run our meetings and study sessions, and we had thought a lot about what a good online interaction should look like. Embarrassingly, we were nerd city about this and had written protocols and processes to help us make every online meeting as valuable and productive as possible. But we were also Luddites. At first, most of us weren't sure what a Breakout Room was, let alone how to use it. There were screen sharing issues. *Wait, which button is it?* If that sounds like you at one point too, well, know that you're safe here.

In other words, while we were studying the transition into online learning, we were also transitioning our own teaching there in fits and starts. This turned out the be a blessing—we got immediate opportunities to apply the things we were seeing in classrooms. Some things proved better than others. We found some tricks that helped. And we also found that there were a lot of tricks that didn't work because they were too clever by half (i.e., they were fancy, but didn't actually make the class that much better) or too complex. Doing them demanded too much of our own working memory to manage—trying to unpack the key scene from the novel, peering into our laptops, and reading in the faces of our participants whether they were with us. We moved slowly but persistently forward, and decided it was more valuable to spend our time learning to do more basic things really, really well than to do flashy things that worked just okay.

Our heads were down, so to speak, focusing on those tasks, when suddenly we looked up and noticed that traffic to the Teach Like a Champion (TLAC) blog had multiplied. People suddenly started writing to ask us to speak at (virtual) conferences on online teaching. We tried to deflect because we knew we weren't experts— *Wow, people must really be at the bottom of the barrel*—but in retrospect, maybe that was the point. We were everyman—well, every teacher—struggling with this challenge, but with the blessing of a lot of video to watch and a room full of teaching nerds to dissect it. We might not be able to give you a theory on online learning, but we sure could cue up videos of amazing teachers to study together. Later, a friend in publishing called and said, "You really need to think about a book. The new school year is coming up fast." First, we laughed. Then we cried. (We were really busy.) And then we got started.

For all our talk of being Luddites, of missing the classroom, and throwing slight shade at technology and online learning (it's out of our system now, promise), we really believe that we—all of us—can get a lot better at this pretty quickly. If nothing else, our own experiences both studying and using these ideas have shown us that, and we'll try to share some of those experiences of getting it wrong and then getting it right throughout the book, and we hope this helps to leave you feeling both motivated and optimistic. It can be done — so it must be done.

With all of that in mind, here's what's ahead.

Chapter 1, by Hannah Solomon and Beth Verrilli, describes a key distinction between two types of online classes, synchronous and asynchronous. We describe some of their strengths and limitations and how to address them. We also discuss how they can work in synergy — how a great lesson might include elements of both.

Chapter 2, by Jen Rugani and Kevin Grijalva, describes "Dissolving the Screen," which is to say, making students feel more connected, remotely. While building and sustaining relationships is an important part of Dissolving the Screen, it's about more than that. It's about doing those things through the content and the craft of teaching — about making students feel connected through learning.

Chapter 3, by Colleen Driggs and Jaimie Brillante, discusses one of the biggest challenges of online learning: distraction. Students are far from us, and they are on screens — a setting that is engineered to offer constant distraction. This chapter is really about how, in online teaching, half of the distraction battle is often wiring your interactions to maximize attention.

Chapter 4, by Hilary Lewis and Brittany Hargrove, is about Pause Points — moments when you ask students to be engaged and active. We get practical and show video of responses to such questions as: How often should Pause Points for active student engagement occur? What kind of tasks are most valuable? How do I do them asynchronously?

Chapter 5, by Emily Badillo, Jen Rugani, and Hannah Solomon, is about assessment — or, as we like to call it, Checking for Understanding. Our students are far away.

We cannot look over their shoulders at their notes or their problem sets. How and when do we attempt to Check for Understanding?

Chapter 6, by Darryl Williams and Dan Cotton, is about the foundational operating systems of any classroom: its procedures and routines—both student facing and teacher facing. The things we do most often are things we should have a right way to do. They are things we should be able to do simply, quickly, and without much thought, so we can focus on learning. This is as true online as off.

Chapter 7, by Rob Richard and John Costello, is about technology and platforms. How can we get as much teaching value as we can out of basic tools? What are some simple hacks to make our lives simpler when we're using technology? How far should we go? Simplicity is our motto.

One of the first things we noticed about Rachel Shin's lesson, that very first day, was how it echoed phrases and actions that recalled the familiar past she and her students had shared. We keep thinking that we can apply that idea in anticipation. That we should set out to plan what we do in our return to brick-and-mortar classrooms to align with what we do online so they echo one another and so we can move easily back and forth between them going forward, as uncertainty will almost assuredly require of us.

In light of all of this, we end with a final reflection on the future and what it may bring. That should prove useful—at least to the degree that it's useful to take advice about the future from people who, here and now, mostly can't find their car keys.

Kidding aside (we've got the keys now!) our goals are twofold: 1) to highlight useful things in small moments in the lives of real teachers so you can make small adaptations to how you teach online, and 2) to show our appreciation for teachers who have been asked to do immensely challenging work in the face of immense uncertainty, and know they must do it well.

Thanks to all of you for your work on behalf of students. It is the most important work in the world.

Chapter 1

Synchronous and Asynchronous Learning

Hannah Solomon and Beth Verrilli

Not all remote lessons are the same, but in general, remote learning takes two forms: asynchronous learning and synchronous learning.

Asynchronous learning happens when the work of learning occurs at different times and in different places — say, when your students fill in a graphic organizer you've posted online and email it back to you, or when you videotape a lecture for your students to watch on their own time. Synchronous learning is the kind that happens at the same time, but in different places. Any kind of class that takes place over Zoom, Google Meet, or any number of platforms qualifies.

Each type of remote instruction has its benefits and limitations. In this chapter, we'll look at each, and offer a few ways to get the most out of both.

ASYNCHRONOUS LEARNING: BENEFITS AND LIMITATIONS

If synchronous lessons are live TV, asynchronous lessons are Netflix (or, more accurately, YouTube). With that difference comes all the benefits of having control over the final product. Since teachers can refilm or edit a video when they find they want to improve some turn of phrase, or wait to begin taping until their own children are napping, asynchronous lessons can produce a higher-quality presentation.

Students, too, have a bit more control in an asynchronous setting. Maybe they need to wait until a sibling is finished with a shared laptop, or log in around their family's work schedules (or their own, in the case of a high school student). They can also watch asynchronous lessons at their own pace, pausing when they need more time to complete a question, or rolling back to hear an explanation a second time.

Asynchronous lessons are also scalable: one teacher can tape a lesson that multiple teachers can use, dividing the content workload among staff and freeing teachers up for other tasks. And asynchronous learning lends itself to more complex assignments, since students can take the time to be more reflective and to put more sustained thought into their work.

We've seen many different ways asynchronous lessons can support student learning. Students might watch a history lecture asynchronously, then use the information to answer a writing prompt offline. Math scholars could watch their teacher demonstrate how to find the average of a series of numbers, then move to practice problems. Asynchronous lessons allow teachers to play with time, too. Lessons can have an "expiration date" or be "evergreen."

Expiration-date lessons are designed to be watched within a specific time frame — as narrow as a few hours or as broad as several days or more. Assigning deadlines is the most common approach ("Watch the lesson and upload the accompanying HW packet before Wednesday at noon," or "Watch the lesson, complete the problem set, and email it to me. When I get it, I'll send you part 2!"), though teachers may also experiment with referring to specific world or community events to bind lessons to a specific point in time. Basing a vocabulary lesson around a class birthday, for example, or selecting news articles to supplement novel study could be included in expiration-date lessons. These types of lessons are especially helpful in establishing and reinforcing responsible work habits in students and in building a strong sense of community.

Unlike lessons with an expiration date, "evergreen" lessons live forever and students can watch them whenever they need to. For example, a teacher might record a quick video on incorporating citations from a primary source if students need a refresher before end-of-unit essays, or simply capture a lesson about three-dimensional prism cross sections without specifying when or how many times to watch it. Students might watch an asynchronously taped science experiment several times.

The internet, too, is full of evergreen videos — famous authors reading their texts aloud, Bill Nye presenting scientific concepts, and Khan Academy coursework — which teachers can use to create a bank of helpful video content. We think as a rule that evergreen videos should be short and pithy, and used primarily for reference, homework, or as introductions to new content (ideally followed up by a video with clearer student accountability and community). Though it may be tempting to imagine recording one video to introduce polynomials every year, student attention and engagement may decrease without those personal and timely touch points.

Asynchronous learning has its downsides, too. For teachers, without the ability to assess the engagement or understanding of their students, even the strongest asynchronous lesson can feel like teaching into a void. And the pressure to make the asynchronous "perfect" might translate into hours of refilming.

On the other side of the screen, students may lose a sense of connectedness to teachers and peers — and feel little accountability during asynchronous learning. We fear that students may watch and politely ignore all of the requests to "Stop and Jot," "add this to your notes," or "complete this problem," and instead wait for the teacher to feed them the right answer as the camera rolls. Or they might industriously complete every task but emerge not having mastered much — and without our knowing it. Without some component of synchronicity or accountability, there is no way of knowing if students are engaged at all. They may press play on the video, doodle on their paper while munching a snack, and then work on the assignment as if they'd never seen it.

For these kinds of engagement challenges, history teacher George Bramley from Brigshaw High School in Leeds, England, shared an elegant solution. George requires students to have a lesson-specific Google Doc open as they watch his prerecorded lecture. Throughout the lesson, he asks students to jot down time-specific notes and answers. Because his questions are set up to be embedded within the content as it is explained (e.g. "What happened before?" "What should King

Harold do next?" "What really did happen next?") and are formative in nature, students can't simply fill in the chart after half-listening. George can tell how attentive students were throughout and assess their lasting takeaways after the video has ended.

George also "checks in" with students during this asynchronous lesson by reminding students where they should be and what they should be doing: "Please make sure you are taking notes about this in that second row of boxes," and "You can type this next bit of information into Box #5." George may not be in the room with the students, but his thoughtful supporting document and verbal reminders ensure that students are processing the information step by step, efficiently and effectively.

There is also the risk that an asynchronous lesson may have asymmetric outcomes: the strong students continue to flourish; the struggling students continue to struggle. Multiple factors can influence those asymmetric outcomes: the attention span of the individual student, how much the student perceives themselves to like or "be good at" the subject, the preexisting relationship with the teacher, and of course the ability and availability of family support.

Consider Sarah, who watches her Spanish lesson while her three siblings run around nearby; she's supposed to help watch them while her mom is out. Amelia, on the other side of town, sits at the kitchen with her mom nearby, keeping a warm but watchful eye on her and helping her stay organized. Who gets more out of that lesson?

As we know from years of making seating charts for our brick-and-mortar classrooms, where you are when you are learning can make a big difference on the outcome. In watching remote learning from around the world, we've seen students "attend" virtual school while wearing pajamas in bed, while buckled in the back of a moving car, and while seated amongst siblings at a crowded kitchen table. We've seen homes where an adult or older sibling is able to sit nearby and refocus a student, and we've peeked into learning environments where it's clear the ninth grader is simultaneously "in algebra class" and managing her much younger siblings.

Both watching a video and completing asynchronous work can require a fair amount of familial support (and internet bandwidth), which we know is particularly challenging for all families—and it's a particularly asynchronous challenge. In asynchronous learning, students are learning in whatever circumstances they may find themselves—supported or independent, confident or insecure.

Finally, too much screen time can increase fatigue and decrease attention. Think of the seven-year-old whose second-grade classroom once burst with song and projects now trying to learn multiplication from two-dimensional Ms. Smith. Or the student whose pull-out classroom gave her the scaffolding and support she needed to succeed in algebra and is now on the same video as all of her classmates. Dwindling attention spans and lack of engagement can seem impossible to manage or monitor online. How do we know the difference between video rolling in the background and students doing the work?

Given the downsides, why even tape asynchronous lessons? Why not just send kids to some educational corner of the internet like Khan Academy where the content is good and comprehensive and ready to roll? A couple of reasons: connection and engagement.

Though a teacher filming in her dining room may lack the slick polish of popular internet fare, human connection with someone who cares about you is indispensable. And engagement, accountability, and task clarity aren't baked into videos not prepared with our own students' learning outcomes in mind. The content of someone else's video is "optional." It simply doesn't have the structure and support. It doesn't remind kids when and where to take notes, or require them to solidify content by pausing to try a problem.

We see both of these—the connection and the engagement—in Joshua Humphrey's asynchronous math class from KIPP St. Louis High School. First, Joshua breaks his daily math instruction into two shorter lessons and provides an assignment to complete in between. Even for adults, it's hard to maintain focus after 60 minutes or more on a Zoom call; by trimming his lessons and providing an application assignment, Humphrey helps his students pace their days, increasing their chances of attentiveness during each lesson. And Mr. Humphrey kept this lesson to a slim 12 minutes. Josh effectively breaks up tasks to help his students manage their cognitive load, applying and consolidating one concept, thus helping to encode it in long-term memory before moving to another. And how much easier it is for students to remain fully engaged when they only have to practice the self-discipline of focus for 12 minutes instead of 40!

Video Clip: Joshua Humphrey, "Reference sheet"

https://www.wiley.com/go/newnormal

Next, as you can see in the clip, Humphrey models two techniques critical to building student investment in asynchronous lessons: he jumps right into the content, and he makes the learning personal.

In online learning, attention is a precious commodity—not a moment should be wasted. By kicking off his class with a clear objective, Josh is able both to keep the whole lesson to under 12 minutes and, even more importantly, signal to students that each of those minutes is important. What's so brilliant about his approach, though, is that he uses this Do Now to reinforce his connection with his students—a connection that is grounded in the learning they do together. He shows his face on the screen, looks directly at the camera, and delivers the directions with Economy of Language, warmth, and just a touch of informality. When he restates the objective "So you've gotta tell me about all the parts [of a polynomial], okay? What do they mean?" in kid-friendly language, it makes his students feel as though they are really back in the classroom with Mr. Humphrey. He reinforces this with his warm smile as he transitions to the Do Now: "First things first, just like in any other [brick-and-mortar] class."

Let's peek into another math class to see similar parallels with younger kids. Just like Joshua, Rachel Shin, of Brooklyn

RISE Charter School, uses every moment of asynchronous instruction to maximize learning and reinforce her relationship with her kindergartners. Rachel, like Josh, maintains the class structure she established in her brick-and-mortar classroom, jumping directly into the daily story problem. She looks directly at the camera with a warm smile, briefly mentioning the rain as a way of building up a tiny bit of challenge: "It's not going to keep us from getting the math done, right?!" Rachel is also deliberate with her Economy of Language, not wasting a single word or second of her students' ability to focus, but her tone is warm and her language informal. Like Josh, she uses time intentionally. She is present and human.

 ## Video Clip: Rachel Shin, "Good morning"

https://www.wiley.com/go/newnormal

Rachel also uses the story problem as an incentive: the student who sends her the best strategy work on their problem is featured in the next day's lesson. This not only makes Nicholas feel incredibly proud that he and his LEGOs are "famous" in class, but also incentivizes his 23 classmates to watch and work hard.

Finally, as Rachel transitions toward her "board" (a piece of chart paper taped to the window), we feel like we are actually in her classroom. She alternates between looking directly at the camera, her students, and at the board, just as she would if they were together.

By infusing their efficient and focused instruction with warmth and presence, both Rachel and Josh are able to make the most of the asynchronous format.

SYNCHRONOUS LEARNING: BENEFITS AND LIMITATIONS

Some of the downsides of asynchronous learning can be addressed through synchronous learning. When done well, a synchronous lesson can truly replicate some of the collegial and engaged mood of a master classroom. Connections can be made and maintained. Students can see their teachers and peers, live, and interact with them in real time. Teachers can once again "read the room," Check for Understanding, and respond to what they see — who is struggling and needs more help. They can know when everyone grasps the concept, so they can increase the pace or present a more challenging problem.

In synchronous learning, there is a much greater likelihood of engagement. Our colleague Colleen shared that her daughter was definitely not a fan of her classes moving online. Until, one day, her teacher Cold Called her. Suddenly, she came alive. She was won over, because she realized that her teacher still sees her, knows she is present, and cares about her answer.

Of course, synchronous lessons have their limitations, too. As teachers, our "home" responsibilities and our "work" responsibilities sometimes collide in ways they haven't before. We've seen lessons where teachers had their own toddlers in their laps, sometimes in tears. (We're pretty sure that wasn't in the original job description!)

Adding further complexity is the fact that getting everyone *to* the lesson *and* logged in at the same time is much trickier than greeting an line of students in the hallway outside. Having to teach through tech adds an additional challenge to the teacher's working memory. A teacher who is juggling all the moving pieces of a lesson — delivering her content, balancing

Means of Participation, comparing student responses to her exemplar, and trying to project warmth and calm — now also has to make room in her brain for troubleshooting tech issues from her kitchen table. It's no wonder that accomplished, veteran teachers may feel as overwhelmed as they did in their first or second year of teaching.

And, as with asynchronous learning, screen fatigue and drifting attention spans sap brainpower. Though it may seem ideal for a fifth grader to spend the hours of 9 a.m. to 3 p.m. online doing synchronous learning with his teachers, we need to consider how many Zoom sessions he can attend in one day without depleting his entire attention span.

	Asynchronous Learning	Synchronous Learning
Benefits	• More polished product • Both teachers and students control their own schedule/pacing • Possibility of more sustained and complex assignments	• Building/maintaining connections • Checking for Understanding and responding to error in real time • Allows for greater engagement
Limits	• Can't assess engagement/understanding in real time • Less connection and less accountability • Disparate impact with struggling students suffering more • Screen fatigue • Decreasing attention	• Coordinating schedules • Tech issues/access disrupt learning • Screen fatigue • Decreasing attention

Though synchronous learning can, on some level, feel most like a classroom, it's not exactly. In fact, many classroom challenges are often magnified through it. How do we assess understanding, or deliver feedback, when we cannot crouch by a student's desk or read over her shoulder? How do teachers effectively monitor student engagement or continue to develop trusting relationships when we—and they—are tiny squares on the screen? These challenges are difficult to surmount, but not impossible. Eric Snider's synchronous lesson on Rita Williams-Garcia's *One Crazy Summer* at Achievement First Iluminar Mayoral Academy (remote) Middle School is the proof.

 ## Video Clip: Eric Snider, "Perspective on poetry"
https://www.wiley.com/go/newnormal

In the lesson, Eric masterfully transitions the best practices from his brick-and-mortar classroom to his synchronous remote instruction. He starts his synchronous lesson just as he would his real class, welcoming each student by name as they pop into the Zoom room—he even shouts out one student's upcoming birthday and another's new hairdo, maintaining the relationships he has already built with his students. They get right into the Do Now, independently reading a three-paragraph interview with the novelist and answering two questions.

Because this is a synchronous lesson, Eric can assess student understanding in real time. Watch Eric do this first by thanking the students as they "chat" their answer to the multiple-choice question; his narration says, "I see your work and it's important" to individual students, but also helps students feel like part of a class, "seeing" their peers hard at work beside them. Then he assesses whole-group understanding by noting that "80% of us got this correct," and proceeds to explicate both the correct and incorrect answer by taking the students back to the text and highlighting the proper evidence. Such a quick feedback loop is only possible in a synchronous lesson, where Eric can assess understanding, diagnose and correct confusion, and make sure all students are set up to succeed as they progress through the lesson.

BUILDING A SYNERGISTIC MODEL

Understanding the differences between the types of learning allows teachers to strategically balance them to maximize student learning. How do synchronous and asynchronous learning support each other? Which is more or less appropriate for students' needs? How can we leverage them in synergy with one another?

Just as teachers do when planning for the traditional brick-and-mortar classroom, they must keep context in mind when deciding how to teach. Variables such as the students' age and abilities, the subject matter, the daily objective, the nature of the content (new material or review), and the time of year (starting the class remotely or moving to remote instruction midway through the year) should guide decisions about when, where, and how to maximize the benefits and minimize the limitations of each type of learning.

The things we love most about teaching seem to transfer best to synchronous instruction. Synchronous lessons seem the best place for establishing and maintaining the trusting academic relationship between students and teacher. Discussion, for example, can only live in a synchronous lesson. Thus, the lessons we usually reserve for discussion and debate, the interactions that peers need with one another to test out and refine their ideas, are synchronous. Challenging material, like a new math concept or an especially tricky reading, also benefit.

Before we jump to an "as much synchronously as possible" model, though, it's important to keep in mind three factors. First, it can be challenging to train or to find the unicorn teacher who both excels at the skills of brick-and-mortar instruction (content delivery, engagement strategies, classroom management) and has the tech savvy it takes to manage screens and platforms to deliver high-quality, engaging, synchronous instruction. Asynchronous instruction allows more room for coaching and feedback before going live — and as many attempts as needed to ensure a high-quality final product.

Second, as we've mentioned, screen fatigue is a real thing, for both teachers and other adults, and for children. It doesn't seem now that students of any age (or their educators, spending their days in multiple hours of professional sessions) can still concentrate fully in the sixth hour of online instruction, no matter how engaging or talented the teacher may be. Asynchronous learning allows for learners to work at different paces. Not only that, but it also allows them to complete their learning tasks fully unplugged — a state with tremendous benefits to attention.

Third, one of the largest benefits and challenges of synchronous instruction is that all players must be present at the same time. If your student population comprises high schoolers who are themselves essential workers, then asynchronous learning becomes a necessity. If you work with a team of teachers, all or most of whom have young or school-aged children at home who are also in virtual school, day-long synchronous instruction may also prove exceptionally challenging. Finding ways to maximize the synergies between asynchronous and synchronous instruction will likely yield the most successful learning outcomes for the greatest number of students.

Our colleagues at Uncommon Schools have explored several potential structures for a hybrid model. In one approach, a lead teacher (department chair or instructional leader) records a single asynchronous lesson that all students watch, whether or not the teacher was their classroom teacher during the school year. For example, an outstanding teacher of seventh-grade science in Boston might record the lesson that all seventh-grade science students in Boston, Newark, and Brooklyn would watch. Students then submit the work from that lesson directly to their own classroom teacher, who provides feedback both in a Google Classroom forum and also via biweekly phone calls. In this way, a variety of synchronous options support asynchronous learning, and human capital is maximized. All students with individualized learning plans, as well as those who need additional assistance, are then scheduled to attend daily small-group synchronous sessions to make sure they progress toward their learning goals. In another synchronous learning support, students who struggled with a particular skill are required to attend a live session in which the challenging material is reexplained and students complete additional practice together. Finally, all teachers offer live "office hours" for their students to attend synchronously. Some students choose to attend these office hours, and others are invited or required to do so by their teacher.

We have also heard of schools providing entirely asynchronous content instruction and offering synchronous opportunities to come together as a community to celebrate success, process challenge, or discuss current events. Many schools have used Deans of Students to facilitate these moments of synchronous community building.

Another way to combine the best of synchronous and asynchronous instruction is to consider a "Flipped Classroom" model, where all instruction takes place via asynchronous video and all "live" time is used for supported practice, discussion, and remediation. In this model, students are responsible for coming to class having watched the asynchronous direct instruction video, at a minimum, and potentially having completed a bit of independent work to serve as a quick way for their teacher to assess their levels of mastery before group practice time.

If you are reading this book as an individual teacher, then these kinds of structural decisions may be out of your control. However, the ideal combination of asynchronous and synchronous learning for your classroom may still be up to you. For that, let's jump back into Eric Snider's *One Crazy Summer* lesson. After the Do Now, Eric plays an audiobook excerpt as students read along, then sets up the independent work—work that will happen asynchronously, but still on the live feed. He stamps this as "the climactic moment" and he's full of questions that make it seem fascinating ("Why does Fern keep barking?") and like a big deal ("Get ready for a plot twist as you now read on your own.").

 ## Video Clip: Eric Snider, "Sync async fusion"

https://www.wiley.com/go/newnormal

Eric's clear-as-a-bell task directions remain on the screen for students as they head off for their independent tasks.

He leverages synchronous instruction to reinforce focus and attention with his warm narration ("I see you Armani.") and asks students to "shoot him a chat" if they need more time. Eric structures the last part of his class as a silent, uninterrupted chunk of time to work, while he monitors what students type in their documents. Ten minutes before class ends, he narrates what he sees: "I see Jazleene typing her answer to our Exit Ticket question . . . so's Jaylee and Jordan D," and "I see Jame, she's going down the text to reread for evidence, really smart, Jame." Eric and his students maintain engagement and accountability to the end and echoes of the classroom abound.

PLANNING: WHAT WAS CRITICAL HAS BECOME CRUCIAL

Planning for remote learning relies on many of the same techniques that classroom teaching relies on. Even so, it's easy to underestimate how much preparation can help set up a teacher for success. True, on the one hand, you don't have to run the overhead projector while the class phone is ringing and Sasha wants to use the bathroom (again!). On the other hand, you'll be trying to teach while also running through a PowerPoint deck, attempting to read student chats, and trying to assess understanding and engagement from tiny boxes on a screen. For this, being ready usually means scripting exemplars, using Economy of Language, pacing appropriately, leveraging Wait Time, varying Means of Participation, and internalizing the lesson before recording or going live. We've found that the importance of the following two planning components is amplified in online learning:

1. **Read your entire lesson plan, even if it was written for brick-and-mortar classrooms.** Though you may

reprioritize and tailor content for virtual learning, that's hard to do correctly without reading the entire plan. Further, in remote instruction, intentional teacher language connecting one lesson to another, or clearly explicating the purpose of a particular activity, becomes all the more important. It's not possible for teachers to make the purpose of a lesson "pop" without having full context themselves — without laying out why it is important and how it is connected to the larger plan.

2. **Complete all student materials as if you were a top student, creating an exemplar packet.** This process helps you to get a full picture of what student mastery will look like, enabling you to guide students there with increased precision. It also is your most valuable tactic to anticipate student misconceptions.

The importance of creating an exemplar is amplified for online learning. When assessing for understanding via "chat" while trying to virtually manage 25 ten-year-olds, you need a crisp and clear exemplar to refer to. Especially if you are delivering asynchronous instruction and don't get to read confused faces or confidently raised hands, you need to have thoroughly anticipated student confusion in advance and preemptively respond to it in your instruction. When you are Cold Calling and listening to students answer through occasionally garbled audio, with competing background noise, or reluctant participation, knowing exactly what constitutes a successful verbal answer is essential. There is no working memory to waste. Being prepared to successfully overcome the unique challenges of remote instruction means starting with deep knowledge of the content you are teaching.

A last element of planning may be particularly critical in remote settings, both synchronous and asynchronous, where the screen plays a much more important role. There's power in using images, but the right design is critical.

In her outstanding book *Teachers vs Tech,* Daisy Christodoulou summarizes two of Richard Mayer's principles of multimedia learning. The first is the split attention effect. Integrating text and images together so that the text appears in small chunks at the appropriate time and place and "narrates" the image allows students to focus their working memory on the most important concepts. It's far more effective than presenting a long description and an image to illustrate it. Integrate the two.

The second principle Christodoulou recommends to teachers is the redundancy principle. Good educational graphics remove all extraneous content to let students focus on what's important. That often means taking images from other sources and simplifying them, rather than merely cutting and pasting them. Joshua Humphrey's math lesson at KIPP St. Louis is a great example. Notice how streamlined his graphics are—how the small highlights appear to support his narration and focus students on the relevant part of his reference sheet.

Video Clip: Joshua Humphrey, "Reference sheet"

https://www.wiley.com/go/newnormal

Once you've thoroughly prepped for the content of your lesson, it's time to focus on your teaching process: how to translate the learning that would have taken place in a classroom to a synchronous or asynchronous setting. It's here that the challenges of effective planning multiply in previously unknown ways. It's important to consider the following:

- Have you determined how you will hold students accountable for doing the work? In other words, how can you be sure that they will really pick up their pencils?

- Have you been intentional about establishing and nourishing the precious back-and-forth teacher-student learning relationship that still exists, despite the screens between us?

- Have you streamlined and prioritized content in response to the real challenge of attentiveness in a remote culture?

Our hope is that the remaining chapters of this book will provide you with structure and context for tackling the unique challenges of planning for virtual instruction.

SYNCHRONOUS AND ASYNCHRONOUS LEARNING: IN REVIEW

In general, remote learning takes two forms: asynchronous (at different times, in different places) and synchronous (at the same time, in the same "place").

- **Asynchronous Learning: Benefits and Limitations:** Asynchronous learning gives teachers more control over the final product, and students more control over when and where they learn. They're also scalable, meaning they can be used across classes. The downsides have to do with a limited ability to assess engagement and to sense connectedness among peers.

- **Synchronous Learning: Benefits and Limitations:** When done well, synchronous lessons can replicate much of the magic of brick-and-mortar classrooms. On the downside, they can be logistically complex, especially for teachers with kids at home.

- **Building a Synergistic Model:** Both types of learning have benefits and limitations. The trick is finding a way to get the most out of both and exploit the natural synergies between the two types of learning.

- **Planning: What Was Critical Has Become Crucial:** Planning is even more important online than it is in person. Being "ready" in remote teaching usually means scripting exemplars, using Economy of Language, pacing appropriately, leveraging Wait Time, varying Means of Participation, and internalizing the lesson before recording or going live.

Chapter 2

Dissolve the Screen

Jen Rugani and Kevin Grijalva

We're happiest when our brick-and-mortar classrooms crackle with intellectual energy built on trust, respect, and community. Gestures of appreciation and acknowledgment—a high five, a star or check next to an exemplar answer, an enthusiastic "great job" when a student corrects a misunderstanding—send our students the message that we recognize their efforts, welcome their participation, and care about their well-being. Inside the four walls of our classrooms, we create spaces of learning where students feel connected to us, and vice versa. Doing so is both critical to student outcomes and one of the most gratifying parts of the job. How, then, do we continue to build and maintain our connections with students when we must leave the four walls of our classrooms behind?

When we cannot inhabit the same physical space, connecting feels harder — and it is. The robust culture that we spend months developing, the millions of connections that form the foundation of our relationships with our students, suddenly seem far away and beyond our grasp. The thousand signals we can send a student through the design of classroom space, the subtleties of our body language, and the influence of their peers are now limited to tiny boxes in the corner of their screen with just our faces visible and their voices often on mute.

When we first shifted to remote learning, the degree to which we would be able to develop and maintain connections with our students was a source of anxiety. We worried about what would happen to classroom cultures and student-teacher connections in virtual schools.

Fortunately, as we started to watch videos of teachers and students adapting to remote learning, we were excited and relieved to see that it *was* possible to build and maintain relationships, even through a computer screen. In some clips we watched, suddenly it was almost like being in a classroom — a bit easier to forget the distance between teacher and student. As we continued to see more and more of these moments of connection, we started to refer to them by using the term "Dissolve the Screen."

To Dissolve the Screen is to heighten and strengthen students' awareness of the back-and-forth exchange that still exists between their teacher and themselves. It's not merely connecting to let kids know that we care about them (though hopefully there is plenty of that). It's establishing a connection through the work so that kids feel both accountable and connected at the same time. Dissolving the Screen conveys a clear message: "I see the work you're doing, and it matters. You contribute to our classroom culture when you take ownership of your learning and succeed. When you're engaged in the work of learning, we are connected because I notice and value your work — and just maybe find happiness in it, too."

It's important to emphasize the focus on connecting academically and through content. One potential pitfall is allowing anxiety about maintaining personal relationships to create environments in which the learning is an afterthought. That is, 30 minutes meant to be a math lesson becomes instead a social video chat with not much accomplished. Ironically, this not only erodes the learning but also the very relationships we sought to prioritize. Unless the purpose of being together is reinforced though teaching, we will not earn students' respect, and that will undermine our ability to build meaningful relationships with them.

While of course there are a variety of ways in which we might demonstrate to students our investment in them and their families (and we'll touch briefly on some ideas in the Beyond the Screen section of this chapter), the most powerful way to communicate our care is by teaching well. Competency is one of the critical ways teachers build trust, so teaching in a way that connects is the key.

Dissolving the Screen is especially crucial in a time when resources for online and video learning are plentiful. While it might be easy to send students a link to a Khan Academy video and call it a day, there's an important difference between getting information via video and feeling like we're part of an online classroom community. There are a lot of ways students can learn online, but Dissolving the Screen is the tool that lets us create vibrant and engaged remote classroom cultures.

Ultimately, this is a leap of faith. We're all still sitting at home in front of our computers, and the distance between us is real. We feel one another's absence even though we're present on screen. Our students feel it to an even greater degree. But Dissolving the Screen reminds them that we're human beings and we're here for them, that we see and appreciate that they're human beings and here for us, and that together we're going to continue to learn.

Successful, Safe, Known: A Framework for Relationships

In recent years, our team has proposed a framework through which to think about building and maintaining student-teacher relationships. We think this is especially valuable in these times of remote learning: When student-teacher relationships are strong, students feel successful, safe, and known.

- Successful: Students connect with teachers who support and push them to feel genuine, authentic success. Authentic achievement is key, as students are astute at distinguishing between empty, easy accomplishments and those that have pushed them to new levels of learning. Trust is a byproduct; it emerges when students feel and believe that the teacher is a capable and competent guide to advancing intellectually and successfully navigating the world of school.

- Safe: Students connect with and believe in teachers that make them and their peers feel physically, emotionally, and intellectually safe.

(Continued)

(Continued)

- Known: Students respond positively and feel connected when the teacher acknowledges and celebrates what's distinct about their work or their identity, and when the teacher sees beyond their current behavior or achievement to see who they are and who they may become.

ECHOES OF THE CLASSROOM

One of the first videos of remote teaching we watched was from Rachel Shin, a kindergarten teacher at Brooklyn RISE Charter School in New York. In this lesson, Rachel is introducing a math story problem for her students to solve. Everything about the clip is warm and reassuring; she's upbeat, familiar, and welcoming, and it feels calming to see her on the screen. Here's a screen shot from her lesson:

She's smiling, of course, but also notice her body language; she leans toward the camera almost as though she were stopping by a student's desk. Watching Rachel on video, it's easy to imagine being in her classroom. Rachel "acts as if" her students are right there in the room with her, even giving them a chance to give her "a big thumbs up" before offering a gentle "good," with a laugh. As she sets students up to solve the problem, she drops in some incentive to keep them watching: "There's one quick challenge at the end of this video, so when you watch the rest, you'll find out what it is!" Rachel sticks to a routine her students know: They will mark up the day's math problem "like we did yesterday together." She even drops into her classroom cadence ("underline my uuuuunits!") to allow her kindergartners to chant along with her as they watch. The leap of faith here is that by offering students something they recognize, they will be more likely to engage and participate.

Video Clip: Rachel Shin, "Math stories"

https://www.wiley.com/go/newnormal

Joshua Humphrey's math lesson from KIPP St. Louis High School is a great example of this idea converted for use with older students. We keep having to remind ourselves as we watch that Joshua is sitting alone in his living room as he tapes this lesson on translating verbal expressions. It feels like he's talking just to you, which reinforces the idea that *even asynchronously, relationships matter*. He's carefully prepared but not overscripted. Joshua's decision to restate the objectives in conversational terms ("*So you've gotta tell me about all the parts [of a polynomial], okay? What do they mean?*") is a powerful example of the sort of thing you might do if you were really in the room with students.

Video Clip: Joshua Humphrey, "Translating verbal expressions"
https://www.wiley.com/go/newnormal

In many of our favorite moments of Dissolve the Screen, the theme that stands out is the feeling of normalcy and continuity. Despite the strangeness of the circumstances, teachers like Rachel and Joshua remind students of the classrooms they once shared (and will share again!). As Joshua introduces the Do Now, he says, "First things first, just like any other class, you all have a Do Now." The context may be different, but there's security and reassurance in the structure. They lift as much as they can from their physical classrooms and bring them to life through their videos. The echoes of their classrooms reverberate through their instruction

Maintaining as much continuity as possible with the brick-and-mortar classroom our students have (in most cases) spent years in can go a long way in helping us Dissolve the Screen for students. Consider ways to set up your teaching space, presentation materials, and student work materials according to familiar systems so that students feel more comfortable and confident to tackle the class work. Even offering images of your handwritten instead of typed notes is an opportunity for connection through familiarity: *There's my teacher's handwriting!*

Beyond the physical setup of space and materials, it's important, as Rachel does, to "act as if" you're in the classroom. You might use consistent verbal and nonverbal cues, dress professionally while filming, or stand while teaching. Sean Reap, an eighth-grade reading teacher at Bedford Stuyvesant Collegiate in Brooklyn, uses a conversational tone as he recaps a chapter of *To Kill a Mockingbird*. He's clearly imagining his students' animated faces as he exclaims, "And then she ate it! Is she crazy?!" Sean draws students in immediately and makes the book seem so engaging; reading it together is a gift. But he doesn't overdo it, and he carries his enthusiasm seamlessly into clear directions to set students up for the day's work.

 ## Video Clip: Sean Reap, "And then she ate it"

https://www.wiley.com/go/newnormal

There's some suspension of disbelief here, especially for older kids — of course Sean and his students both know that this isn't really a conversation, just as Rachel's students may or may not really give their screen a big thumbs up. But we think there's value in putting in the extra effort to "show up" (just as we would in our brick-and-mortar classrooms) to increase engagement, connect through content, and magnify the impact of our remote teaching.

SEEING STUDENTS AND THEIR WORK

Bringing elements from our physical classrooms into our remote ones is only one aspect of dissolving the screen to create connection. In our brick-and-mortar classrooms, one of the most powerful tools we have to connect is our ability to "take the temperature" of the learning and culture in the room. In person, we normally rely on hundreds of subtle cues—shifts in body language, a change in a facial expression—to help us gauge the success or struggle of our students. We circulate and monitor their answers during independent work time. We provide feedback and adjust our instruction accordingly. In a remote setting, it's much harder to "read the room" and see in real time where students are succeeding and struggling.

In order to connect with our students through their work in a remote setting, we need to find ways to more effectively "see" them and their effort. This means we must engineer the learning environment to maximize our ability to monitor students' thinking and learning so that we can respond supportively and effectively. This is challenging in synchronous settings, when our students appear through a tiny window on the screen, and doubly so in asynchronous learning when we quite literally cannot see them. Following are a few best practices we've collected when thinking about engineering our online classrooms to better "see" students and their work.

Synchronous Learning. In a synchronous setting, it's important to use all of the tools at your disposal. Just as in physical classrooms, sometimes it takes using multiple tools and techniques across a lesson to get the full picture.

- **Camera On, Face Visible:** Setting an expectation that students keep their cameras on, with their face visible, not only allows us to see our students but allows them to see each other. This can reinforce the sense of connection in a virtual classroom and create both community and accountability for students. During whole-group discussions, consider pausing a screen share and shifting to "gallery view" so that as many faces as possible are visible at once. This allows you and your students to speak directly to one another and can also help you more easily notice visual cues that allow you to assess the tenor of the discussion. Maybe you shout out a student who has been nodding along with the discussion, or Cold Call a student who keeps going on and off mute but seems hesitant to step forward with their idea.

- **Private/Public Chat:** The chat feature found in many online learning platforms can help optimize the legibility of learning in a variety of ways. Public chats, or chats to everyone, allow both you and your students to see thinking happen in real time and create a record of thought that everyone can refer to later. Private chats between you and individual students are useful in providing a space for students to think in writing without fear of embarrassment while allowing you to provide individual feedback. For younger students or less confident typists, consider designing prompts that ask for just one word or phrase in response.

- **Polls:** Some programs have tools that allow you to create polls for students to respond to with the click of a button, which is a great high-tech option for taking a pulse check of your class. We also love low-tech solutions that can be particularly useful with young students (e.g. "Show me thumbs up or down, do you agree with what your classmate said?" "Put up one finger for answer A, two fingers for answer B, or three fingers for answer C.").

- **Show Me:** Another relatively low-tech option to make student thinking visible is to use the technique Show Me, in which students work independently on a piece of paper or mini-whiteboard and then hold their work up to the camera.

Asynchronous Learning. Seeing student thinking in response to an asynchronous lesson relies upon students sending us artifacts of that thinking. When engineering the learning environment, then, we need to maximize the likelihood that students will want to engage in and submit the tasks we ask them to. You might consider:

- **Varying Submission Methods:** Vary the ways in which you ask students to submit work. Students might text you a response, snap a picture of their handwritten work, send an email, record a voice memo, and so on. You might choose to offer multiple submission options for the same task based on students' access to tech. Offering variety can also prevent work submission from becoming stale and help you better manage the influx of messages.

- **Ask Self-Reflective Questions:** In addition to content-driven questions ("Text me your response to question #4"), self-reflective questions ("Send me an email with an area you've made progress in and something you're still struggling with") can be just as valuable in helping us understand the class's progress and "take the temperature" of the learning.

- **Use Challenge:** Provide challenges or incentives so that students *want* to show you what they've done. Our colleague Kim Griffith does this beautifully in an asynchronous Retrieval Practice quiz. Even her very first words ("Okay, team") communicate a sense of togetherness and perhaps a bit of competition, and she brings a kind of game-show-host energy to the task. ("Let's see how many you can get correct. Here goes!") At the end of the clip, she challenges students: "Keep this score so that the next time we do this Retrieval Practice, you either match or exceed that score. I can't wait to see what's next." This is a powerful way not only to communicate the importance of owning one's own learning, but also to reinforce predictability and accountability. We'll be doing this again, Kim makes clear, and it's important to keep track of your work. After watching Kim's clip, one teacher remarked, "Kim doesn't just Dissolve the Screen—she explodes it!" Rachel Shin provides another example of asynchronous Challenge when she tells her kindergartners that the first person who sends in their work will be featured in the following day's lesson. Note that Rachel is incentivizing completion, not necessarily accuracy, subtly implying that what she values is the effort—incorrect work will be just as valuable as correct work.

Video Clip: Kim Griffith, "The bourgeoisie"

https://www.wiley.com/go/newnormal

Video Clip: Rachel Shin, "LEGO"

https://www.wiley.com/go/newnormal

ACKNOWLEDGE AND RESPOND

Once we create an environment that allows us to see our students and their work, we need to acknowledge their efforts. Students are far more likely to disconnect—both literally and figuratively—if we are constantly asking them to produce work that we fail to recognize. There are a few techniques from the brick-and-mortar world that we think are especially useful online to let students know that we see and appreciate their efforts.

- **Narrate the Positive:** In order to build and sustain momentum in a remote class setting, it's useful to name and acknowledge students who are meeting and exceeding your expectations. Eric Snider demonstrates the power of positive narration in his synchronous reading lesson with his fifth graders at Achievement First Iluminar Mayoral Academy Middle School in Cranston, Rhode Island. Eric's students are reading *One Crazy Summer* by Rita Williams-Garcia, and Eric follows a section of reading with a series of comprehension checks. As soon as he asks students to engage, he starts to give quick verbal appreciation for the participation he sees: "Thanks Lisa, thanks Juwaun, thanks Elsie." He makes students feel seen when they work hard, and he normalizes active engagement by helping students see it all around them. Narrate the Positive works in asynchronous lessons, too, when teachers name and appreciate students who have submitted strong work or demonstrably engaged with the learning since the last lesson.

Video Clip: Eric Snider, "Delphine feels proud"

https://www.wiley.com/go/newnormal

- **Acknowledge versus Praise:** It's important to keep a healthy balance between acknowledgment and praise. It may be tempting, in these difficult circumstances, to go above and beyond in heaping praise on our students for their contributions. But just as in our physical classrooms, overpraising for routine behaviors dilutes the power of true praise and can inadvertently communicate a low bar for participation. Eric Snider's video highlights the difference quite well: While he thanks every student for their participation, notice how he praises Armani: "I appreciate the message, thanks buddy. That's above and beyond." This moment is more special for Armani because he can trust that Eric's praise is genuine and earned.

- **Strategic Cold Call:** Even when your students log into your virtual classroom, it is easy for them to feel anonymous. Does my teacher know I'm here? Does she care? Would it make a difference if I logged off, or checked my phone? Using Cold Call throughout your lesson not only holds students accountable but also reassures them that we value their presence and their contributions.

When Cold Calling, consider using language that is explicitly positive and inclusive. We can signal our interest in the student and their ideas with phrases like, "Maggie, I'd love to know what you think about this passage," or "Maggie, you always have such interesting insights around problem-solving. What strategy did you use here?" You might even incorporate your knowledge of your students' personal interests into your Cold Call: "Maggie, I know you're an animal lover. What was your reaction to the description of the horse and its rider in this part of the book?"

Beyond acknowledging students' effort, the ways in which we respond to student work can reinforce connection and help develop warmth within our remote-classroom culture. By generating positive feedback loops around student work—even and especially when that work is incorrect—we create an environment where students *want* to engage and participate with enthusiasm. Here are some of the tools that we see excellent teachers using online to create this kind of engagement:

- **Show Call:** Show Calling excellent student work by putting it onscreen for all to see is a powerful way to build positive feedback loops. It sends the message to students that despite the limitations presented in a remote setting, you still care about the quality of their work and will highlight strong efforts made by your students. Ben Esser of Achievement First East New York Middle School demonstrates the power of Show Call to start his asynchronous sixth-grade reading lesson. The lesson starts fast as he describes the reading to come: "A king gets toppled today," Ben begins, hitting the ground running. It feels purposeful right from the start and honors students' time by getting started right away. After just 18 seconds, we're "snapping it up" for people who got a "perfect" score on yesterday's classwork. Then Ben doubles and even triples down on the idea, shouting out kids whose classwork average is high and then showing the "really exemplary Exit Tickets" a couple of students wrote.

Exemplary Exit Tickets

Rachel ▮▮▮'s Compound-Complex-Appositive Masterpiece:
Although some may say the execution of Hickey, a guard of Washington who was planning to kill him, was just, Hickey did deserve to die for plotting to kill General Washington, but he shouldn't have been killed publicly for everyone to see him struggle like that.

Taylen ▮▮▮ Vocabulary Extravaganza:
While Hickey's punishment was cruel and tormenting, it was just due to him nearly trying to assassinate George Washington and becoming a pariah to his nation as a result.

Video Clip: Ben Esser, "Appositive masterpiece"

https://www.wiley.com/go/newnormal

The message here is important; while Ben is a less immediate presence in his students' life, he still sees and values their work. The work matters and the work connects them. It may come as little surprise that Ben also uses a version of Show Call when working synchronously with students by leveraging the private chat function. As students chat private responses to him, he zeroes in on a "truly excellent answer," then copies and pastes that answer into the public chat so the whole class can read it. It's a quick but powerful way to highlight student effort and lift the learning of the group.

- **Feedback:** Providing concrete, timely feedback remains a crucial part of effective teaching, even when doing so remotely. Making sure that feedback is personal ("You explained your solution to #3 using strong math vocabulary"), not generic ("Great work!"), can build trust and respect by communicating that you've not simply looked for the correct response, but you've noticed the individual effort put in by the student.

- **Transparency:** We can let students know we value their time and attention by being transparent about the ways in which their work has informed our instructional decision-making. You might open a lesson by saying, "We had planned to push forward to our next topic today, but I noticed yesterday we seemed to struggle with remainders, so I've put together a few more practice problems to help us really nail this." In an asynchronous lesson, you might offer options for transparent differentiation: "If you got both Exit Ticket questions right yesterday, skip ahead three minutes in the video. If you missed at least one of those questions, keep watching so we can walk through an exemplar response."

- **Culture of Error:** Coaching students through error can do as much to Dissolve the Screen and connect with students as celebrating strong work. When we create virtual classrooms where error is not only acceptable but encouraged as part of the learning process, it sends a powerful message to students that we are there to teach, not simply to lecture at our screens. Acknowledging and embracing error says to our students, "I see you, I'm here to help you, and I will celebrate our progress together."

BEYOND THE SCREEN

We recognize that connecting with students beyond the virtual classroom is important, too. There's synergy between our personal relationships with students and our academic connections with them. When we know our students personally, we can embed this into our academic work with them to Dissolve the Screen and make them feel seen in a way that is special and specific.

Rachel Shin provides a beautiful example of this idea. Her student Nicholas has submitted excellent math work, so she opens the next day's lesson by highlighting him personally in that day's problem: "Today's problem is actually brought to you by Nicholas. I'm going to talk about Nicholas, and his favorite thing in the world today . . . LEGOs!" Rachel's knowledge of

Nicholas and his interests makes the story problem special and specific to who he is as both a human being and a student.

Video Clip: Rachel Shin, "LEGO"

https://www.wiley.com/go/newnormal

Some other ways to connect beyond the screen include:

- Phone calls or texting one-on-one, depending on the age of your students, can be quick and easy ways to check in. One of our colleagues has found that teacher FaceTimes are a particularly useful motivator for her students.

- If possible, try a socially distanced visit. Consider having a student read to you from across a driveway or on opposite sides of a stoop.

- Informal, small-group video chats can help restore the peer-to-peer connections that are so important in school but that we are deprived of in a remote setting. Facilitating student connection can help foster culture (and depending on the age group, you could be present during the chat or not).

- Consider planning, or offering students the chance to plan, class activities through video chats. We've heard of and seen events like virtual spirit week, trivia, show and tell, or any other activity that allows students to share more of their personalities.

- Families are a vital part of the learning community in any setting, and remote learning makes the family-teacher connection even more impactful. Consider how and when you might schedule family-facing communication to reinforce the school-home link and communicate that we're in this together.

- Interest and feedback surveys can be a helpful way to provide kids a platform to communicate with you about themselves and their experiences during this time. Not only can this provide useful information to guide your instruction, but it can also help kids feel that their input about the shape and direction of their new learning environment is heard and appreciated.

Building Connections from a Remote Start

The future of the coming school year is uncertain. While some doors will open again this fall, it's likely that many schools will incorporate at least some type of remote learning into their instructional plans. Teachers will face the challenge, then, not just of maintaining existing connections but of creating them with new students. How does one build relationships in a 2-D space with 2-D strangers?

This is uncharted territory for the vast majority of educators. As you embark on the coming year, we know you will adapt and improve upon the ideas you see below. We hope these suggestions provide useful starting points as you work to establish a culture of connection and exchange in your remote classrooms.

- Before the year begins, schedule a 1:1 video chat with each new student.

- Develop a list of questions to discuss with students about the upcoming year. How did you feel about online learning in the spring? What did you like? What did you find challenging? What are you hoping to accomplish this year? These, among others, can give valuable insight to help you shape your class culture.

- Record a short video introducing yourself, your "classroom" space, and (if applicable) a preview of the content. You may also ask students to send you a video introduction in response.

- Safety permitting, do a socially distanced class meet-up or schedule socially distanced house visits. Reinforcing the idea that we are actual people in a class together can go a long way toward fostering a positive classroom culture in the beginning of the year.

- If possible, consider looping up a grade with your students to leverage existing relationships; school leaders might find flexible staffing models to be especially useful in the coming year.

DISSOLVE THE SCREEN: IN REVIEW

- To "Dissolve the Screen" is to minimize the medium and bring forward the back-and-forth between teacher and students. It's really about establishing a connection through the work that makes kids feel both accountable and connected at the same time.

- **Echoes of the Classroom:** One theme that stands out in successful remote "classrooms" is the feeling of normalcy and continuity. Despite the strangeness of the circumstances, great teachers remind students of the classrooms they once shared (and will share again!) with their physical setup, as well as verbal and nonverbal cues.

- **Seeing Students and Their Work:** In order to connect with our students through their work in a remote setting, we need to find ways to more effectively "see" them and their effort. We must engineer the learning environment to maximize visibility of students' thinking and learning.

- **Acknowledge and Respond:** Once we create an environment that allows us to see our students and their work, we need to make a point of acknowledging their efforts. Students are far more likely to disconnect—both literally and figuratively—if we constantly ask them to produce work we never recognize.

- **Beyond the Screen:** Connecting with students beyond the virtual classroom is important, too. There's synergy between our personal relationships with students and our academic connections with them. When we know our students personally, we can make them feel seen in a way that is special and specific to them.

Chapter 3

Culture of Attention and Engagement
Colleen Driggs and Jaime Brillante

In every classroom, building a strong culture of attention and engagement is critical. In an online "classroom," where students interact through devices often designed to distract, it is doubly important—and doubly difficult to accomplish. That is the fundamental battle of remote teaching: distraction is always just a click away.

In *Why Don't Students Like School?*, Daniel Willingham describes the function of working memory and long-term memory and the impact each has on learning. Working memory, he explains, plays the most active role in learning and higher-order thinking. Because of it, critical thinking happens. Thanks to working memory, we have *Hamlet*, penicillin, and the theory of relativity.

But working memory also has its limitations. If working memory is overloaded, the quality of our output begins to decline—or we simply don't retain new information as well. Working memory comes in limited supply, and we have to be careful to preserve it.

Long-term memory, on the other hand, is nearly unlimited, and recalling information encoded in long-term memory is often critical to the insights working memory provides. Not only that, but the more you learn about a given topic, the more connections you build, and the better you remember things about that topic. To preserve limited amounts of working memory and to aid in encoding, then, it's critical to provide students with opportunities to consolidate their knowledge and begin transferring it to long-term memory.

Working memory also affects perception—what you're able to notice about a sunset, say, or a data set. If working memory is overloaded, perception decreases. Take driving your car, for instance. If you're on your phone (even hands-free), you are far more likely have an accident than if the road has your full attention. A simple phone conversation with your partner about the grocery list increases the odds that you'll misjudge the rate of approach of an oncoming car—not because your hands are busy, but because your working memory is.

The challenges of working memory—both in terms of encoding and perception—are complicated by an online learning environment. In *Teachers vs Tech?*, Daisy Christodoulou points out that students almost always have both a laptop and a phone accessible in remote work environments, which encourages them to "multitask" even more. The daughter of a colleague described how obvious this has been to her in her online classes. "I look at the screen during my Zoom calls and I can see the blue light shining up at so many of [my classmates'] faces. I can tell they're on their phones but my teachers don't (or can't) look closely enough to see it."

Christodoulou cites a 2016 study by Carter, Greenberg, and Walker, in which students were allowed to bring devices to some course sections but not others. Not surprisingly, students performed better in the sections with no devices. Additionally, Christodoulou notes that in studies monitoring undergraduate media use during class, one found "94% of [students] used email during the lecture and 61% used instant messaging. Another similar study found that in a 100-minute lecture on average students spent 37 minutes on non-course-related websites."[1]

Christodoulou goes on to describe the detrimental effects of "multitasking" on our working memory. She argues that research suggests that we can't actually multitask. Instead, we switch quickly back and forth among tasks. This kind of task switching "makes performance [on competing tasks] slower and more error prone...and reduces the working memory resources going toward the topic being studied."[2] Essentially, working memory is overloaded with multiple tasks, making consolidation and encoding efforts futile.

Citing a study showing that undergraduates typically switch from one window to another in their browsers every 19 seconds, Christodoulou writes, "When we use a connected device, we are using a device that is plugged in to a distraction engine."[3] This distractedness becomes a habit for us as soon as we are on our devices. Our brains are adaptable and neuroplastic. They are changed by the way we use them and habituated to the context. Over time, writes Maryanne Wolf, skimming replaces reading, and our capacity to concentrate is eroded.[4]

On the flip side, underloading working memory isn't great, either. If students aren't engaged, they get bored, start to check out, and growth slows. All of this is magnified in an online environment, with their screens open and things like TikTok competing for their attention.

Whether it happens in person or online, learning relies on working memory to process ideas and encode concepts in long-term memory. It's easily overloaded and underloaded—meaning that if students don't get a chance to consolidate new concepts in engaging ways, they'll struggle to remember and will tire quickly. An ideal online lesson includes multiple short activities to keep students engaged and give them a chance to consolidate regularly. This is harder online, but it's doable. Building a culture of attentiveness and engagement online relies on delivering content and designing activities so that students' working memory is neither overloaded nor underloaded. In this chapter, we'll look at some models for getting the most out of working memory by building attentiveness and preventing distraction.

BUILDING ATTENTIVENESS AND PREVENTING DISTRACTION FROM THE START

Successful online attentiveness in synchronous and asynchronous lessons is contingent upon students' ability to attend to, interact with, and engage in a singular task online. In a synchronous lesson, this looks like students equipped with materials for note-taking, looking actively at the screen, and prepared to ask and answer questions. While impossible to observe in an asynchronous setting, teachers can use a short Rollout to describe habits of attentiveness and invest students in building them.

It's worth noting that a foundational condition to attentiveness is an organized workspace—one devoted to online learning, ideally free of phones.

Beyond the workstation setup, strong starts are important. Students (and adults) typically associate online learning with passivity. Think about how just hearing the word "webinar" conjures up memories of hours spent sitting passively in front of a screen, on the receiving end of an overwhelming amount of information.

Without a focused start, even adults can devolve into passivity. In our first online PD, participants didn't speak until 22 minutes into the session. We asked them to use the chat function on Zoom, but we realized they needed to speak first to normalize participation in the same way we do at our in-person workshops. The next day we had them participate verbally on the first slide to signal the value of their engagement and the expectations for the duration of the session.

For students, a crisp and clear kickoff is even more important. Students need clarity about what it means to be a student in this new context (e.g., "You'll need a pencil and a notebook so please have those ready"). Young people tend to read slow, meandering starts as indications of the teachers' low value on or expectations for their time together. To them, it feels like "not really school." And it's hard to come back to class from a start that feels like recess.

So start warmly, brightly, and with humanity, but start *quickly*. Get down to business. Get students doing something right away. Show that you value their time and prevent underloading their working memory. Give clear, decisive directions. You may briefly remind students of procedures and expectations ("Cameras on, please") and aim to have them actively completing a task within the first three minutes of the lesson.

For example, watch how Joshua Humphrey, math teacher at KIPP St. Louis High School, introduces the objectives for the day and then transitions immediately to the Do Now—all in an asynchronous lesson. Take particular note of Joshua's Pacing. Even though his introduction is personalized, it's also incredibly efficient. Joshua is all about value. He's not wasting time as he moves directly to the Do Now and asks students to get to work.

Video Clip: Joshua Humphrey, "Reference sheet"

https://www.wiley.com/go/newnormal

Here is another example of an effective introduction. It's from Year One teacher Amanda Moloney at Ballarat Clarendon College in Victoria, Australia. In her brief lesson intro, she warmly greets students, quickly sets expectations for the lesson, and then immediately transitions into her lesson on measurement.

Video Clip: Amanda Moloney, "You're in the right spot"

https://www.wiley.com/go/newnormal

Students are still unsure about what this new form of learning means. Show them that time online has value. From the outset, set the norm that their lesson will be purposeful and productive, requiring their full engagement and attention. Start the lesson with frequent, small circuit tests to socialize attention, and embed them throughout the course of your time with students. Here are some examples of tasks you might request in a synchronous lesson:

- "Thumbs up if you see my screen."
- "On your fingers, how many more minutes do you need?"
- "Give Alicia some shine."
- "Just chat me the word 'ready' when you've finished the problem."

As much as you can, ask students to use raised hands or thumbs up instead of chatting you or clicking one more thing to demonstrate their attentiveness. It builds human connection and pushes teachers to look at kids' faces rather than an additional digital tool.

MATERIALS AND SYSTEMS TO SUPPORT ENGAGEMENT

In an online setting, learning materials take on a whole new importance. The materials you present for online instruction—both synchronously and asynchronously—are central to supporting student engagement and learning. Creating clear, simple materials with the right balance of text and imagery will enable students to devote as much of their working memory to learning lesson content as possible.

Daisy Christodoulou has a number of principles to maximize learning by designing graphics to sustain focus and hone working memory. In *Teachers vs Tech?*, she cites Richard Mayer's findings that, if we show text and images together, working memory is better able to connect them, contributing to better understanding. Christodoulou goes on to explain that the pairing of visuals and text is even more impactful when the words that describe a given image are placed alongside it. Here's an example of how Jen Rugani applied this idea to her *Lord of the Flies* lesson. To supply students with critical background knowledge for understanding the novel's setting, she chose two images and paired each with a short caption to describe the image.

lagoon: a pool of water separated from the sea by a sandbank

pink granite: a common type of rock formed by hardened lava

Christodoulou also gives guidance on what Mayer and team have called the redundancy principle. By removing extraneous content, good educational graphics focus students on what is most relevant, thereby reducing strain on working memory. A clear visual field is key to maintaining engagement and clarity. Take a look at the Do Now from Joshua Humphrey's math class. Here, he uses animations to highlight answers as he reviews problems, drawing student attention to what's most important both visually and verbally. This simple use of multimedia supports students in efficient processing and maximal learning.

Do Now

1. Which of the following shows the statement 4 less than 12?	2. Which of the following shows 3 less than an unknown value?
a. $4 - 12$ b. $12 + 4$ c. **$12 - 4$** d. $4 + 12$	a. **$x - 3$** b. $x + 3$ c. $3 - x$ d. $3 + x$
3. Which of the following shows double the sum of 8 and 4? a. $2 + 8 + 4$ ⟸ Common mistake b. $2(8 + 4)$ c. $2 \cdot 8 - 4$ d. $2(8 - 4)$	STAMP IT: Write the expression which shows three times the value of 5 less than 12.

Designing materials with clear What to Do directions can help students follow along with lesson activities without having to ask for clarification or losing attention completely. Whether you are using asynchronous or synchronous instruction, there will always be those moments—the doorbell rings, a text comes through, or the dog barks—when we will lose our students' attention. Student-facing materials should have clear instructions to help them stay on track (or get back on track after a disruption).

The same principles that apply for brick-and-mortar classrooms apply online. What to Do directions should be bite-sized, sequential, measurable, and observable. Of course, in the remote world, directions vary depending on content and student age. For example, watch Alonzo Hall and Linda Frazier from Uncommon School's math team. They're both great examples of teachers who reinforce clear directions both verbally and visually. Both teachers highlight important directions in yellow so students notice them. Alonzo even makes thistransparent to students: "Whenever the yellow highlight comes across our page it is simply a reminder that you can/should pause the video to copy the notes from the page." Linda reminds students of the importance of her visuals by saying, "Please pause to make your paper look like mine."

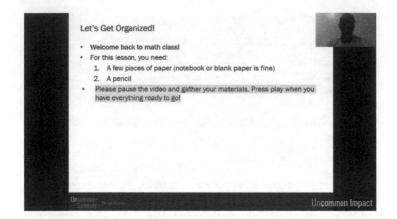

Video Clip: Alonzo Hall and Linda Frazier, "Let's get organized"

https://www.wiley.com/go/newnormal

Alonzo and Linda also highlight the power of shared systems across teachers, especially online. The more familiar and more consistent the directions are, the more students will get used to them and the more successful they will be. The consistency between approaches says: We are still a school; we're still connected. It also builds upon what we know about working memory and long-term memory. Repeated use of systems consolidates in long-term memory, freeing up the working memory.

One of our favorite clips showing clear What to Do directions is this lesson, created by TLAC's very own Kim Griffith. Here she narrates her What to Do directions as she displays a simple image of the loose-leaf paper her students are labeling. As students work to complete their Retrieval Practice questions, Kim posts a timer (the golden circle in the corner of the slide). This simple visual helps students attend to their Pacing while keeping the screen free from distraction. She uses simple color-coding to help students attend to the key terms in the day's review. Without the ability to see her students and confirm their understanding, simplicity is key to student success.

In another variation for elementary school students, Rachel Shin creates a visual field that closely represents her classroom (one that her first graders are no doubt familiar with). Rachel uses her window as an easel and stands alongside her math problem. Students see their teacher and the math problem side by side, just as they would if they were seated on their rainbow carpet back in their classroom. Again, Rachel uses simple color-coding to support student understanding and help students focus on the key parts of the work as she narrates.

These teachers show the power of a simple visual field coupled with clear, concise narration.

SHIFTING LESSON ACTIVITIES: SUPPORTING PACING AND CONSOLIDATION

Maintain the momentum and energy you build at the outset by incorporating a variety of types of tasks in pursuit of your lesson objective throughout the lesson. In brick-and-mortar classrooms, we discuss the value of inserting mileposts throughout the course of the lesson. These reference points along the route make the distance covered more visible to travelers. We can do this online by planning a series of shifting activities in pursuit of a lesson objective. Consider, for example, the activities in an online middle school ELA lesson — a lesson designed to take about 90 minutes, with the objective of "examining Golding's enchanting yet ominous depiction of the island" in *Lord of the Flies*. The lesson looks like this:

- Complete Do Now: Students respond in writing to a prompt based on excerpts from the previous day's reading.

- Review Do Now: After listening to/watching the teacher review some key ideas and share some additional knowledge, students update their notes to reflect new understandings.

- Vocabulary Instruction: The teacher introduces two new words and definitions, then asks students to complete a series of questions (in writing and orally) to reinforce their new word knowledge.

- Reading-Cycle 1: Students read *Lord of the Flies*, pp. 11–12, independently with an annotation focus.

- Writing: Students respond to a Stop and Jot question in their notebook, using their new reading and vocabulary to craft a carefully designed sentence reflecting their new understandings.

- Writing Review: After listening to/watching the teacher review some possible answers to the Stop and Jot question, students revise their answers.

- Reading Cycle 2: Students read *Lord of the Flies*, pp. 13–14, together with the teacher with an annotation focus.

- Writing: Students respond to a Stop and Jot question #2 in their notebook analyzing three lifted details.

- Writing Review: After listening to/watching the teacher review some possible answers to the Stop and Jot question #2, students revise their answers to include key ideas

- Reading Cycle 3: Students read *Lord of the Flies,* pp. 14–17, together with the teacher with an annotation focus.

- Writing: Students respond to a Stop and Jot question #3 in their notebook, analyzing a key quote from the text.

- Writing Review: After listening to/watching the teacher review some possible answers to the Stop and Jot question #3, students revise their answers to include the key ideas.

- Final Writing Task: Students will respond to a question via email using at least one detail from your text. When finished, students will email their answers to their teacher.

Each time the activity changes, it's a milepost for students signaling the forward progress of their lesson. Using Pacing tools like Brighten Lines makes the mileposts pop so students feel like there is a constant, dynamic variety of ever-changing activities rather than a steady drone of online sameness. Teachers can Brighten Lines by naming the next task with simple slides, or by adding phrases like "Meet me at page 14 for our next reading cycle." Switching tasks this way helps students better see the switches.

Incidentally, several of the lesson activities described above — especially those involving writing and annotation — also support knowledge consolidation. Shifting activities also prevents working memory overload (and prevents the kind of underload that often leads to distraction).

Means of Participation is an academic system that helps students understand how they are expected to participate so that teachers can manage participation successfully. In brick-and-mortar classrooms, transparent and explicit expectations allow us to ensure "voice equity" and depth of thinking. Means of Participation is also critically important to maintaining focus and attention (see Chapter 6 for a full discussion and some video examples).

Simple circuit tests will never be fully sufficient. At the end of the day, what we're really striving for is a constant circuit of real thinking.

BUILDING ATTENTIVENESS AND ENGAGEMENT WITHIN LESSON ACTIVITIES

Shifting between lesson activities can promote attentiveness and engagement, but it's also worth thinking a bit more deeply about building attentiveness and engagement within activities, too. Let's look at two common lesson activities — reading and writing — and consider how we can adapt them to maximize attentiveness and engagement in an online setting.

Writing and Note-Taking. A significant body of research demonstrates the benefits of writing notes by hand. From increased focus to improving memory to stimulating creativity, the list of benefits is substantial. We recognize the logistical benefits (and necessity) of asking students to submit typed responses. But that doesn't mean that every note they take, response they write, or problem they solve has to be typed. Consider encouraging (or requiring) students to handwrite notes throughout the lesson, jotting their reflections, or solving a problem set with a pencil.

For many students, a typed submission signals finality—an endpoint—whereas handwritten notes feel like safe places to "think in writing" and to see ideas as formative. Handwritten notes are useful for lowering the stakes of writing for all students, especially the most reluctant. By asking students to jot their responses with pencil and paper, we can implicitly encourage them to take risks and signal the value of their thinking and idea development. In order to maximize accountability for handwritten notes or responses, ask students to email or text you a picture of their work. Below we see the model Jen Rugani creates for her students as they prepare to take notes while reading *Lord of the Flies*.

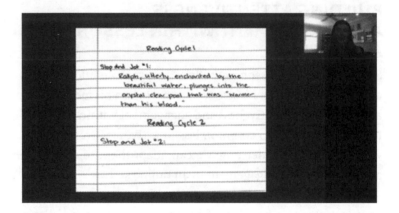

Reading. In any classroom setting, there are three primary ways of reading: Teacher Read Aloud, Whole Class Shared Reading, and Independent Reading. In physical classrooms, one of the most important is Teacher Read Aloud. We believe this to be true for all classrooms, not just elementary classes. In an online classroom, Read Aloud has potential to have all the captivating power of an audiobook, but one that has come to life, annotated and targeted specifically to a class of students.

In this first video clip, Jen Rugani reads *Doctor De Soto*, William Steig's story of a clever mouse dentist. Jen models shifts in mood and highlights crucial words so students build vocabulary. Her joy and pleasure in the tale help her surmount the added challenge of maintaining student focus in an online world.

Video Clip: Jen Rugani, "Doctor De Soto"

https://www.wiley.com/go/newnormal

Jen carefully manages her young listeners' attention—telling them what to pay attention to and where to put their eyes as they toggle between the text and her screen presence. She makes sure they are reading as much as listening. She starts by explicitly telling her students to focus on the word "one." After a moment's pause, Jen is off, reading through two pages of text, her pauses as rich as her reading. Critically, she reads the text slowly enough to let students process and feel every word. Suddenly, Jen interrupts the text with an excited, "Oooh, readers!" and the directions to "Put your eyes on me." It's impossible for students not to follow through, when Jen is so excited.

Jen sustains and directs student attention throughout her Read Aloud. Her reading mimics the voices of characters, completed with shouting, whispering, and weeping. Her voice layers in meaning, punching each word in De Soto's risky decisions to "let the fox in" or exhaling in relief when the fox reveals that he was "just joking" as he snaps his jaws shut. Jen makes her students feel like they are sitting in a circle with her, reading together in real time.

We see much of the same happening in Sean Reap's eighth-grade English class. Older students may need fewer reminders to track, but they still benefit from hearing challenging texts come alive. In this section of *To Kill a Mockingbird*, Sean tackles the narrative voice of Scout Finch in subtle yet skillful ways. His reading of "hearty" *sounds* hearty, and he pauses at each comma to model how complex syntax should sound. Sean can send his mature readers off to finish reading on their own, set up for success through his initial Read Aloud. In a moment in time where screens loom large, we are glad that they can capture the voices of our teacher-readers.

Shared reading also has significant benefits. Control the Game is a system for engineering students' oral reading to make it productive, accountable, and efficient. It helps to build a culture where students love reading and read a lot. With some small adaptations, it's a technique that works (almost) as well online as in the classroom. Watch how Arrianna Chop from Libertas College Prep leads a shared reading with her (grade level) students as they read and enjoy a passage from Pam Muñoz Ryan's novel *Esperanza Rising*.

Video Clip: Arrianna Chopp, "Officially getting started"

https://www.wiley.com/go/newnormal

Before reading, Arrianna provides a focal point for reading by keeping in mind Mama's sickness caused by the dust storm. She then ensures that all students attend to the same place in the text by sharing her screen and highlighting the sections they're reading. Like the teachers in the Read Aloud videos, she breathes life into the text and builds engagement through her own expressive reading. When students are Cold Called to read, they seamlessly pick up, demonstrating that they're following along carefully. After a short segment of reading, Arrianna asks students to shift to a writing prompt to give students a chance to reflect on and consolidate what they've just read.

ANTIDOTES AND DOSAGES

Let's face it, we've all had Zoom fatigue: staring into the screen, droopy-eyed, counting the minutes until you hit the alluring red "Leave" button. Even if something is valuable, the dosage matters. Too much of a good thing is no longer a good thing.

Why all the exhaustion? After all, being at home allows us to teach and learn in cozy pajama pants, snug on the couch. Shouldn't this be easier than the classroom? According to Gianpiero Petriglieri, an associate professor at INSEAD, being on a video call requires more focus than face-to-face chat does. In video chats, we actually need to work harder to process non-verbal cues—things like facial expressions, the tone and pitch of the voice, and body language. And paying more attention to these cues consumes a lot of energy. "Our minds are together when our bodies feel we're not. That dissonance, which causes people to have conflicting feelings, is exhausting. You cannot relax into the conversation naturally," he says.[5] Knowing that Zoom fatigue is a real challenge for educators and students, teachers can make choices to help prevent the mental exhaustion that comes with constant video conferencing.

One way to avoid Zoom fatigue is through the use of "antidotes" to too much screen time. In other words, offline time.

Some student activities should have antidote characteristics: either be not-screened or even anti-screen.

Sometimes or maybe even much of the time, we recommend kids read a physical book, write pencil-to-paper, or listen to a book on tape when they aren't in highest-use screen-based meetings. While asynchronous video has its place, low-tech, screen-free asynchronous activities can help combat screen fatigue. And could it be that they might even be better for learning?

Could "Write in your journal for 30 minutes. Take a picture and text it to me," be better than "Type a one-page response and submit it via Google Docs"? Could "Read the chapter and record yourself reading your favorite ten sentences aloud" be a good counterweight to screen, screen, screen, all day in your bedroom? Yes, in fact, we think it is, and some teachers have done a great job showing just that.

Reflect back (or even better, flip back) to the outline of Jen's *Lord of the Flies* lesson from earlier in this chapter. Throughout the lesson, students respond to the reading by jotting in their notebooks in response to various questions. These answers are then discussed and revised throughout the lesson. It isn't until the final lesson task that Jen asks her students to type a response via email and send along for review. In this way, she combines low-tech opportunities with formative writing tasks to provide short breaks from the screen, thus preventing the Zoom fatigue that could too easily accompany a 90-minute lesson.

More than varying tasks to include antidotes, Zoom fatigue can also be combated by variations in scheduling. As you plan your lessons, ask yourself: How much screen time is appropriate for my students? How can I best balance breaks from screen time with the connections provided in synchronous lessons?

Joshua Humphrey of KIPP St. Louis utilizes an entirely asynchronous model—one in which students watch two short lessons per day, then complete a brief assessment applying the covered skills. Just the idea of keeping asynchronous lessons short and breaking in half was a really good takeaway in and of itself. Dividing up on-screen tasks into shorter chunks and punctuating them with off-screen tasks (and possibly a break) can help students sustain their pace. When they begin a second session of the day, it is with fresh eyes and renewed energy.

In this next video, Eric Snider leverages the synergies of asynchronous and synchronous instruction in what we think might be a "best of both worlds" approach.

Video Clip: Eric Snider, "Sync async fusion"

https://www.wiley.com/go/newnormal

The idea is that you could kick off class with a short synchronous lesson—say, 20 sharp and engaging minutes. Then you could assign work for students to complete asynchronously while still "on the line." In this way, students still get time to work independently, and it becomes possible for you to occasionally check in with individuals or simply say, "I'm here if you need me," like live office hours. You could let students turn their cameras off, or you could provide some soft accountability—as you'll see Eric do—by having them leave them on. At the end, you could bring everyone back together to review answers.

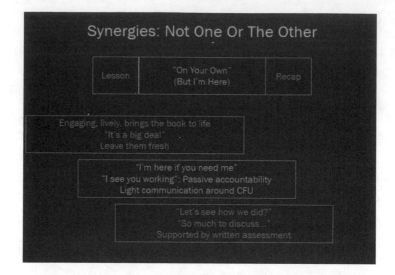

Synergies: Not One Or The Other

| Lesson | "On Your Own" (But I'm Here) | Recap |

Engaging, lively, brings the book to life
"It's a big deal"
Leave them fresh

"I'm here if you need me"
"I see you working": Passive accountability
Light communication around CFU

"Let's see how we did?"
"So much to discuss..."
Supported by written assessment

Here's how Eric did that in a recent lesson on Rita Williams-Garcia's *One Crazy Summer*. The video starts with Eric playing the audiobook to his students. Then he sets up the independent work: it's the climactic moment and he's full of questions that make it seem fascinating ("Why does Fern keep barking?") and important ("Get ready for a plot twist as you now read on your own.").

Eric's task directions remain on the screen, and he then reinforces focused and attentive behavior: "I see Armani." At the end we hear Eric ask students to "shoot him a chat" if they need more time, taking advantage of his ability to assess where they are in real time.

CULTURE OF ATTENTION AND ENGAGEMENT: IN REVIEW

Building a strong culture of attention and engagement is especially critical in an online "classroom," where students interact through devices often designed to distract. The fundamental challenge of remote teaching is this: distraction is always just a click away.

- **Building Attentiveness and Preventing Distraction from the Start:** Successful online attentiveness is contingent upon students' ability to attend to, interact with, and engage in a singular task online. To set students up for success, an ideal workstation setup and clear, quick lesson starts are key.

- **Materials and Systems to Support Engagement:** Creating clear, simple materials with the right balance of text and imagery will enable students to devote as much of their working memory to learning lesson content as possible. What to Do directions should be bite-sized, sequential, measurable, and observable. The more familiar and more consistent directions are, even across classrooms, the more successful they will be.

- **Shifting Lesson Activities: Supporting Pacing and Consolidation:** To maintain the momentum and energy you build at the start, use a variety of types of tasks aligned with your objective throughout the lesson. Online, we can best do this by planning a series of shifting activities that build on each other in pursuit of a lesson objective.

- **Building Attentiveness and Engagement Within Lesson Activities:** Building attentiveness and engagement within activities is crucial, too, especially in an online environment, thinking through the best ways to maximize attention in reading and writing.

- **Antidotes and Dosages:** There is such a thing as too much of a good thing. Zoom is no exception, and Zoom fatigue is real. A good way to avoid Zoom fatigue is through the use of screen time "antidotes," or other approaches that have antidote characteristics. Get kids reading books, writing on physical paper, and diving in to any number of not-screened or anti-screen activities.

Chapter 4

Pause Points
Hilary Lewis and Brittany Hargrove

Our crash course in online learning involved both studying video and trying things out ourselves. In retrospect, this turned out to be something of a gift.

After a few months of studying online teaching, we began to run trainings ourselves. We ran one particular series of sessions for a group of teachers from St. Louis. We believed that the content was strong. We had video clips of great teachers in action, and we'd spent the days leading up to the first session planning. We had prepared the key things to point out and the right questions to ask.

The questions were especially important. We wanted our participants to be engaged and active and we wanted to be intentional about using, and calling attention to, the replicable moves teachers made in their videos so that other teachers could copy them and adapt them. Frequently, throughout the first session, we incorporated opportunities for participants to talk with us and to one another, to write and think about the content in different ways. The design of the session felt solid.

But as we studied the film afterward, something felt "off." We couldn't help but watch the clock. From the moment we began the session to the time we first asked participants to do something (to share their thoughts by typing initial impressions of a video into the chat), eight full minutes had elapsed. When we asked them to write, people began slowly and hesitantly. They seemed mildly surprised and a bit reluctant. Perhaps not everyone had heard the directions. As facilitators and teachers, we began to think about whether our directions were strong enough, whether our questions made sense, whether they were with us or not.

From there, we worked hard to build a more dynamic culture in the session, providing frequent opportunities to participate. We made sure to share and respond to participants' comments to show how important they were. Things definitely improved, but we had to work harder than we'd expected to get the energy to where we wanted it. It never quite felt like our in-person sessions do.

At the next session, using the same material, we made one small change. We made it our goal for people to participate sooner. Within three minutes of the session's start, we asked participants to respond to a short, thought-provoking question by writing their thoughts in the chat. Enthusiasm for this exercise was noticeably different this time around. As soon as we asked, we could hear keyboards clicking away. The responses were fresh. The insights were excellent. Several people even commented a second time.

And it wasn't just the first exercise that changed. Participants were more energetic and engaged throughout the entire session. From that point on, they seemed to expect to participate—they were waiting to. The whole session changed, all because there was no 8-minute precedent of passivity to overcome. It turns out that all participants needed to feel invested and a part of the conversation was a full, running start.

We are used to being passive online. We log on and the first thing we might do is turn our cameras off—confirming in a way that we are only there as a passive observer. Maybe we switch tabs or have a look around the internet. Or we open up an email to send post-meeting so we don't forget to send it. Or we're trying our hardest, but we're struggling to focus. We begin to tune out despite ourselves. In that sense we're a lot like our students.

As teachers, if we don't engage people right away, then we allow these processes to continue unchecked. Participants grow more and more passive. After 10 minutes, you get half the participation you would if you asked the first question in 5 minutes. After 20, screen names start to pop up as cameras go off.

What is a good rule of thumb for a brick-and-mortar classroom—get people active and interactive early—is more like an Iron Law of Online Learning: Continuously engage people actively throughout the session and include a task that requires everyone to respond (in the chat or in a Breakout Room) within the first 3 minutes. In the most successful lessons we've watched since, we've seen this law borne out reliably.

Not only do teachers get a stronger, more enthusiastic response from students when they incorporate frequent short pauses to interact and reflect and engage, both in synchronous and asynchronous settings, but how soon those interactions start is also critical. We are always fighting the tide of passivity, reminding students of how active online classes require them to be. If there is one critical term to understand to make online learning more effective, it's "Pause Points," our name for short, interactive moments embedded in a lesson.

PAUSE POINTS: EARLY AND OFTEN

Online teaching, whether synchronous or asynchronous, should pause frequently—at least every five minutes—for some kind of active engagement to ensure that students feel invited into the lesson and so they become involved and invested.

You can see Joshua Humphrey make this shift in his lesson at KIPP St. Louis. He starts with the objective, describing what students will be doing. Seconds later, he transitions into the Do Now. It's time for action. His students pause and answer five quick questions. Even though the lesson is asynchronous, he's doing everything he can to make sure the pace is fast and the activities frequent.

Video Clip 6: Joshua Humphrey
https://www.wiley.com/go/newnormal

Short, frequent Pause Points send a clear message: you'll be actively involved. But they do more than that. They are also important from the perspective of both working memory and attention. To consolidate knowledge and engage in content are critical in online settings.

Recall that working memory is what we use when we are conscious of thinking. The site of problem-solving and higher-order thinking, it is powerful, but it is also limited and easily overtaxed. Try to reread the previous paragraph and rewrite it in another document or an email. How far can you get without forgetting words or having to go back to check again? Four or five words? Maybe six or seven? This is an indication that your working memory is maxed out. When that happens, you stop being able to remember new things. Your ability to execute skills is reduced. So is your perception. So you need to take opportunities to refresh your working memory.

The way to refresh working memory is to do something with an idea. Think about it. Talk about it. Even a few seconds begins the process of consolidating it into long-term memory, which begins to free up working memory for new content. You can keep talking and talking in other words, but you're getting diminishing marginal returns from everything you say unless you pause and say, "Chat with a partner. What are some connections you're making?" or "Jot down some initial responses to the story," or "Now that you know how to do these problems, let's try one."

Furthermore, as a wide variety of research has shown, as soon as students (well, people) get connected to the internet, their attention starts to fracture. On a computer, the typical undergraduate (i.e., a presumably successful student) switches browser windows every 19 seconds. Left to their own devices, people will drown in their own devices. So don't leave them idle on a connected setting. Force them to engage actively, over and over. You will make the thread of instruction more compelling—and make it harder to go window hopping.

FOUR PURPOSES OF PAUSE POINTS

The Pause Points we embed in our lessons should be engaging, even if they are often brief. That said, not all Pause Points should be the same, and Pause Points should serve at least four purposes: they should 1) build a culture of cognitive engagement and accountability, 2) allow for formative thinking, 3) enable us to Check for Understanding, and 4) provide an opportunity to consolidate learning into memory via retrieval practice.

1. Build a Culture of Cognitive Engagement and Accountability. It's critical to build a culture that establishes the expectations for active engagement and the habit of follow-through. One way to build in accountability, both in synchronous and asynchronous settings, might be to stamp the learning by having students do what we call a Stop and Jot. For instance, in a lesson on the geographical features of Mesopotamia, a teacher may say, "What are the advantages and disadvantages of living in Mesopotamia? Pause the video now and write down at least two advantages and two disadvantages." To take it a step further, the teacher can acknowledge that the student completed the task in a very simple way. Before showcasing her notes, the teacher might say something like, "Welcome back! Let's compare your list to mine."

In an asynchronous setting, the risk with these kinds of pauses is roll-through — when students either accidentally roll through the pause and skip the work or deliberately decide not to pause and skip the work, like any unattended 14-year-old is likely tempted to do. A good but obviously not failproof solution here is to use a visual cue and some awkward silence. Take Chloe Hykin at Marine Academy Plymouth, for example. She and her colleagues thought very carefully about this problem, and solved it by throwing a bright, clear "pause" sign onto her slides when it's time to pause the video. Not only that, but she often leaves a fair amount of dead time — a clear reminder to students that they should be pausing. It's effective, and students are less likely to roll through by accident.

In a synchronous setting, teachers can create an active environment in a few ways, such as by having students share their responses to a rich question with everyone in the chat box. The feed of responses that comes through when student share their response with the whole class is a great way to push habits of discussion.

Alternately, a teacher might choose to ask her students to first think privately and write notes with pencil and paper. For example, the teacher might ask, "Did the benefits of living in Mesopotamia outweigh the costs? Take the next 60 seconds to jot down your ideas in your notebook." With that move, she's done a few things. She has prepared students to have strong ideas if they're asked to participate; she has made it easier for herself to ask students to share their thinking; and she has socialized students to use a non-device-based tool to process the session. She has also introduced some variation to the lesson and caused her students to use a means of processing ideas that they'll have a record of (and that, research suggests, they'll remember better).

But it's not always an either/or choice. A teacher could almost as easily combine the two forms of writing, asking, "Did the benefits of living in Mesopotamia outweigh the costs? Take the next 60 seconds to jot down your ideas in your notebook." At the end of the 60 seconds, she might add, "I am going to ask you to share one of your ideas in the chat." This way, it's not just two rounds of engagement holding students accountable for active involvement, but *two different types* of involvement: first, a round of informal thinking in the form of a personal brainstorm, then a selection and refinement of one idea to share with others. Using different types of involvement can really help support a culture of cognitive engagement and accountability.

It's also important to note that one of the weaknesses of synchronous instruction is our ability (or inability) to really go deep on ideas. There's only so much students can write in the chat. But layering different Pause Points (e.g., first write informally, then share, then go to a Breakout Room and discuss one response that you select) and connecting them, we can achieve something closer to the deep dives of the physical classroom.

The idea of asking students to engage the content in a variety of ways in short bursts with pauses spaced throughout the session applies to both synchronous and asynchronous environments, even if the tools of the asynchronous session and your ability to see follow-through are more limited. Using consistent tools across the two types of setting can help. For example,

Amanda Moloney of Ballarat Clarendon College in Victoria, Australia, included mini-whiteboards on her materials slide for an asynchronous lesson, just as she would in a synchronous one.

WHAT YOU WILL NEED

- Maths grid book
- Grey lead and red pencil
- Mini whiteboard
- Whiteboard marker and eraser

She'll ask students to use it to answer questions throughout. Here's an example:

LESSON STARTER 1   MINI WHITEBOARDS

• 35, 40, 45, 50, 55, 60, 65
  +5   +5 +5

• 2s backwards from 30 to 0

• 4s from 4 to 48

Using mini-whiteboards allows little hands to erase quickly and easily. It also allows Amanda to create an example in PPT that looks at lot like what they are working on. More than that, in assigning the use of white boards in her asynchronous lessons, she's reinforcing a habit used in synchronous lessons. In a sense, she's saying that, even though she's not watching students complete asynchronous lessons, they carry the same weight and should be approached with the same tools as if she were.

Synchronously, asking students to do work on mini-whiteboards and hold them up to their screens expands the range of what they can write and share. From math problems to diagrams to spelling and vocabulary, the list of possibilities is endless. It also makes student writing bigger and therefore easier to share: "Jason, hold up your whiteboard and we'll all study your work and be ready to evaluate." Using whiteboards in both settings makes them a consistent habit that students are comfortable and familiar with.

There are also many simple tools to build a culture of accountability. In our Systems and Routines investigation (Chapter 6), we discuss the importance of having "cameras on." Once you've done that, you can ask for all sorts of tiny visual responses. "Thumbs up when you've finished reading the passage," or "Raise your hand if you had a similar response to Bethany." Even interactions as simple as these can connect the circuit and help keep students engaged and active. This is just one of the reasons we prefer having students raise a physical hand on screen rather than using a digital hand as some platforms allow. Physical hand raising is also more immediate. It happens right away and it feels more human and personal. When we respond to them, "Okay, some people need a bit more time. I'll give you a few more seconds," or "Yeah, I had the same response to Bethany's idea," we communicate, "I see you, I see you working hard, and I value your participation."

2. **Allow Formative Thinking Among Students**. In the previous section, we described a teacher asking her students, "Did the benefits of living in Mesopotamia outweigh the costs? Take the next 60 seconds to jot down your ideas in your notebook. I am going to ask you to share one of your ideas in the chat." Doing this provides another opportunity that is especially valuable: the opportunity for formative thinking among students.

After this sequence, the teacher might ask students to read their peers' takeaways in the chat and discuss or respond verbally. In other words, the Pause Point would end with students responding to and developing *one another's ideas.*

In remote learning, students are not only isolated from you, their teacher. They are also isolated from their classmates and from one another's ideas. Using Pause Points to break down this isolation—to put their own developing ideas in conversation with their peers'—is critical for cognitive engagement and formative thinking.

For instance, take this video of Arrianna Chopp from Libertas College Prep in Los Angeles, California. In it, she and her students engage in a discussion about the novel *Esperanza Rising.* Watch how Arrianna first pushes students to think in writing before they move to discussion. First, Arrianna makes reference to earlier inferences the students had made. "Two chapters ago, you all said that she [Esperanza] is becoming a dynamic character." She then asks, "How is she becoming a dynamic character—a character who is changing? Please take one minute to write it in the comments." After the comments come flying through the chat, Arrianna facilitates a discussion. Notice the way her students build off of one another's thinking—evidence of strong habits of discussion and a vibrant peer-to-peer culture.

Video Clip: Arrianna Chopp, "Las Ciruelas"

https://www.wiley.com/go/newnormal

Pause Points for formative thinking can also work in asynchronous settings. A teacher might ask, "What geographic features may have attracted nomads to settle in Mesopotamia? Pause the video now and add your thoughts to my Google Classroom post." Students would then be able to see their peers' responses to the teacher's Google Classroom post and edit or add to their initial response. To see how they're doing—and to incorporate new ideas into their own thinking—students need to compare their answers to their peers.

In a synchronous lesson, a teacher might post the same question, but instead use a student's written response as a prompt for a discussion. It could even be from the previous day's homework—"Let me show you something very thoughtful that Kalia wrote. I want to ask you to reflect on it."—or from participation in the moment—say, a comment selected from the chat or harvested from a shared Google Sheet. (Imagine an online version of a Show Call). Students could discuss their peers' ideas in Breakout Rooms, or through their own written responses. As with the technique Show Call in brick-and-mortar classrooms, we strongly suggest sharing written work, because written work is permanent. It allows students to examine and revisit it carefully. (And one of the best concluding activities for a discussion is to ask students to revise their original statement to reflect what they've learned.)

3. **Check for Understanding**. Checking for Understanding is arguably more challenging when we are teaching

remotely. And since our teaching needs to change based on the degree to which students have understood what we taught, it's also equally important in an online setting, if not more so. And even though Checking for Understanding is the primary topic of the next chapter, we can't help but note here that Pause Points make for great opportunities to get a read on how much your students understand.

In one synchronous example, Eric Snider from Achievement First Iluminar Mayoral Academy Middle School in Rhode Island is teaching the novel *One Crazy Summer*. Shortly after a reading, he uses a Pause Point to ask a question—to do a "quick Check [for Understanding]." He wants to gather data on where his students are, so he asks them to chat him their answers. As he reviews the chat, he's looking less for comments to build and reflect on and more for a sense of the big picture: do they understand? If they do, how many of them do? If they don't, what mistakes are they making?

Video Clip: Eric Snider, "Delphine feels proud"

https://www.wiley.com/go/newnormal

After his analysis, Eric reveals that the class is split. Seeing the need to remediate, he talks through why one of the incorrect answer choices was wrong, eliminating this choice for the class. His next move is to have the class go back to their answer choices, reevaluate the evidence, and select the best possible answer from there. He does not presume that his explanation automatically resolved the issue. And in fact, his follow-up reveals the opposite. Students are still confused. But simply knowing there's a problem creates an opportunity to address it. And it only took a moment of Pause for Eric to gain this insight.

When it comes to Checking for Understanding, frequency is critical. Good teachers make a habit of regularly checking throughout the session. Setting an expectation about these kinds of short interactions around content being normal creates lots of opportunities to assess and respond. Pause Points make it easy and natural for these kinds of Checks to regularly punctuate your lessons.

Not only is frequency important, but so too is Checking early on in the lesson. If students don't understand something, you want to know right away. This moment is from the very beginning of Eric's lesson. As you'll see in the clip, students are very often able to help one another. Here Eric relies on Solaree to explain the solution to her peers. It highlights a wonderful moment, and a teaching strategy that works a lot more effectively when Pause Points are a regular part of your lessons—when students are already in the habit of listening to and valuing one another's ideas.

In an asynchronous setting, the teacher moves to Check for Understanding are similar, but the feedback loop lags. Students share their understanding through sending a photo of their work, submitting a Google Doc, or filming a video of them orally sharing their reflections, just to name a few. So while teachers can still tap into student understanding, the analysis comes after the fact, rather than in the moment.

From a Pause Points perspective, George Bramley's lesson at Brigshaw High School in Leeds, England, is a work of art. As the Google Sheet his students fill out shows, he's planned dozens of short interactions for different sorts of activities: note-taking, reacting, and predicting. After they turn this doc in, George will have all the data he needs to get a clear sense of how well students understood the core ideas of his lesson. But sometimes all that data is even more than you need, and looking at 30 answers times however many Pause Points can quickly become unwieldy. In that case, you might consider a representative sampling.

Video Clip 19: George Bramley

https://www.wiley.com/go/newnormal

Let's say your asynchronous lesson has six or seven Pause Points where you ask students to pause and complete work or respond to ideas. At the end of the video you could then say, "Great. I'd like to see your work from questions two and five from today's session. Please email me [or text me a picture of, or answer on the Google Sheet] those questions." This way, students still have an incentive to do all of the work, but your marking load is a bit more manageable.

We know that online learning can be limiting. In an asynchronous setting, we are taking a leap of faith with our Pause Points. And while we are trusting that our students are not rolling through our videos just to catch the gist of the lesson, we are also not naive. To better ensure students do the work of asynchronous lessons, it's incredibly important to embed Pause Points, and to diversify what you ask of students at any given moment. To aid in building that accountability through the screen, you might use the pause symbol to indicate when to pause your videos, display a timer, and let that run in real time while students reflect, or try working "alongside" your students.

We also understand that, especially in an asynchronous setting, the teacher may not realize there is a student misunderstanding until much later than they might if they were with their students in the classroom. The same may be true in a synchronous setting. To combat this, it is imperative to close the feedback loop. When students can compare their answers to a teacher exemplar, whether that is in real time or through an assessment graded later, there is a more comprehensive understanding of what the student knows.

4. **Use Retrieval Practice.** As several recent important books exploring findings in cognitive science — including Daniel Willingham's *Why Don't Students Like School?* and Peter Brown, Henry Roediger, and Mark McDaniel's *Make it Stick* — have described, long-term memory is much more important than most teachers realize. Most of what students learn, they forget. The nineteenth-century German psychologist Hermann Ebbinghaus first documented the relentlessness and reliability with which we forget what we learn. He charted it on something called a "forgetting

curve." A day after learning something we have often forgotten more than half of it, even under ideal conditions. But online learning isn't ideal conditions and, although no one has charted a comparative forgetting curve for things learned online, it's likely that they are even steeper given the fact that most learning functions are less effective there. It's easy to overlook, but one of the best things to do in a Pause Point is to spend a few minutes doing a bit of retrieval practice, where students recall and reapply previously mastered content. This video of our colleague Emily Badillo using retrieval practice to reinforce key ideas during a lesson on *Animal Farm* as part of our Reading Reconsidered English curriculum is a good example.

Video Clip 20: Emily Badillo

https://www.wiley.com/go/newnormal

Emily does a great job of "Dissolving the Screen," and creating a gamelike atmosphere. She uses the timer and countdowns to add a playful urgency to the exercise. It feels gamified. We love how she doesn't ask students to press pause as they work. The exercises are timed, so Emily keeps the clock running "live," making the whole thing feel a bit more engaging. And of course, Emily adds an Accountability Loop to close out the exercise. Not only does she ask students to self-score, but she asks them to text her a picture of their work, using this Pause Point not only for student retrieval practice but to Check their Understanding.

In what can sometimes feel like a constant stream of online time, Pause Points can even serve a bonus fifth purpose — to break up the monotony of the day. We know that teaching through a screen is no match for the vibrant variety of the in-person classroom, but there are things you can do to ensure your lessons don't come across with all the passion of "webinars for students." Pause Points allow for little moments of insight, of connection, and of variety—in your day, and your students' day. So use them, because it seems safe to assume that we could all use a little more of all of those things.

PAUSE POINTS: IN REVIEW

- "Pause Points" are short, interactive moments embedded in a lesson. They can and should take a variety of forms.

- **Pause Points: Early and Often.** When teaching remotely (synchronously or asynchronously), it's important to pause often to actively engage. Beyond sending the message that students need to be on their toes, short, frequent breaks are also important for preserving working memory and attention—both critical in remote settings.

- **Four Purposes of Pause Points.** Pause Points serve at least four purposes: they 1) build a culture of cognitive engagement and accountability, 2) allow for formative thinking, 3) enable us to Check for Understanding, and 4) provide an opportunity to consolidate learning into memory via retrieval practice. They also help break up the day.

Chapter 5

Accountability Loops and Checking for Understanding

Emily Badillo, Jen Rugani,
and Hannah Solomon

Checking for understanding is at the heart of teaching and learning. To do our job as effectively as possible, we need to constantly know what students think and how that thinking changes over the course of the lesson. To paraphrase John Wooden, our goal is to recognize the difference between "I taught it" and "They learned it." This is one of the more significant challenges of teaching, even when we're all in the same room with our students. When we're all online, the challenges multiply.

In the classroom, we assess students understanding by reading over their shoulders, observing their reactions, and listening in on discussions. While assessments can help us see the gap between teaching and learning at the end of a lesson, checking for understanding throughout a lesson allows teachers to effectively "read the room," getting a sense of students' ideas and misconceptions as they arise. Students can much better reach mastery if we spot misunderstandings as they emerge and then find the best way to address them. And because misunderstandings tend to snowball and become more entrenched, recognizing and addressing them quickly is essential.

But online, things are different. Our touch points with students are limited, which makes checking for understanding more difficult that it already is. Suddenly, we find ourselves without many of the informal tools we would rely on in the immersive, collective experience of the classroom. There is no reading over the shoulder of students miles away, and it's hard to truly tune in to a person's affect and body language through the tiny window of a Zoom call or an emailed submission after class. And our lesson may not even be live. We may have recorded it alone in our living rooms, sent it out to students, and hoped for the best. In all of the conversations we have had with teachers since the classroom moved online, the same question comes up again and again: "How do I know that students are doing the work and to what degree they're succeeding?"

We've seen many successful teachers Check for Understanding through "assessment loops" — moments when teachers ask students to complete a task that will be assessed against an exemplar in some way, either by the teacher or by the students themselves. For teachers, assessment loops are a way to collect data and monitor student understanding; for students, assessment loops create frequent opportunities to consolidate understanding and develop self-assessment skills. They also help create a culture of collective accountability—a culture in which students feel both responsible for completing their work and confident that doing so will improve their learning.

We have seen teachers use three specific types of assessment loops to check understanding: Implicit Assessment, Real-Time Assessment, and Lagging Assessment. As each type has its benefits and limitations, to get the most complete picture of student understanding, a balanced approach is best.

IMPLICIT ASSESSMENT

Implicit Assessment involves students checking their work against a model, usually with the understanding that the work will not be submitted. During a lesson, teachers might pause to allow students to complete a short assignment, then share an exemplar, highlight common errors, and/or explain how students should have arrived at the correct answer. As they do so, teachers use language that conveys to students a responsibility for self-assessment and revision: "Make sure to correct any mistakes," or "Be sure to revise your responses to add anything that was missing." While we see this most commonly in asynchronous lessons, synchronous lessons may also include moments of Implicit Assessment in the interest of time or increase student ownership of their learning.

Let's consider a moment of Implicit Assessment from Joshua Humphrey's high school algebra class at KIPP St. Louis. In this asynchronous video, students are asked to pause the video to complete the Do Now independently. Afterward, Joshua reviews, using simple animations to highlight the correct answers. Students are not going to submit their work to Joshua, but they will need to understand these concepts to complete work that comes later in class. The pace is quick—Joshua spends less than two minutes reviewing the Do Now, and he encourages students to check their own answers. On one tricky question, Joshua briefly explains a common wrong answer before revealing the right one. He says, "Number 3, the common distractor on this one was A...but the key word they said in here is the sum...so we have to use parentheses." His animations highlight first the error, then the correct response, helping students both to check their work and to recognize a common mistake. Even online in an asynchronous setting, creating these kinds of opportunities for students to see and correct errors themselves makes error analysis a valuable tool for CFU.

Video Clip 21: Joshua Humphrey

https://www.wiley.com/go/newnormal

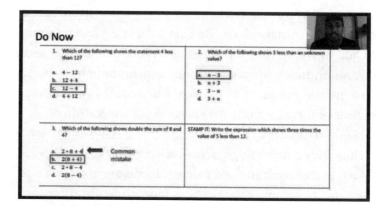

Seth Kumar-Hull, a fifth-grade teacher at Creo College Prep in the Bronx, follows a Pause Point during reading with a moment of Implicit Assessment. It's an asynchronous lesson, and students are reading an embedded nonfiction text about the Danish Resistance to support their understanding of Lois Lowry's *Number the Stars*. Seth reads the text aloud, then pauses after the first paragraph and says, "Your jot here will be explaining, what is the big idea of this section? Try to use the word 'perilous' in your jot. 30 seconds, pause, go."

Video Clip 22: Seth Kumar-Hull

https://www.wiley.com/go/newnormal

After allowing a moment for students to pause the video and make their annotations, Seth begins again. "Check to see that your jot is something similar to mine. I said that the Danes thought that it was too perilous to get involved in another war." He then enters his idea in another note-taking document, modeling the process he wants students to follow and giving students a clear exemplar for their own work.

While we typically associate Implicit Assessment with written work, in an early elementary lesson, these moments may also be spoken aloud. For example, in Davis Piper's first-grade lesson at Brooklyn RISE Charter School, Davis uses flashcards to review sight words with students. For each word, he shows the card, says the word twice, and pauses for students to say the word to themselves. On tricky words, he repeats the pronunciation so students can hear the difference between the word they said aloud and the way Davis reads it.

Normalizing Error and Revision

Implicit Assessment loops offer opportunities both to normalize error and to build good habits around revision into the culture of your classes. In one of our

(Continued)

(Continued)

favorite clips from Marine Academy Plymouth in Plymouth, England, Chloe Hykin does just that.

Throughout her video, Chloe frequently reminds students that if they are struggling, they can get support—and where to get it. "If you're having a look at these two questions here, splitting ratios, and you can't remember how to do it or you're not 100 percent sure, stop the video now and watch that Level 2 video. If you're feeling confident...get ready for our Retrieval Practice quiz." This way, students can proceed based on their own self-assessment of their understanding.

Video Clip 23: Chloe Hykin

https://www.wiley.com/go/newnormal

This level of optionality both helps to normalize error and struggle—students are encouraged to monitor their own understanding and make informed choices about how best to proceed—and offers a concrete action that students can take to revise beyond just correcting their responses.

In another video from Marine Academy Plymouth, Jen Brimming leads an asynchronous high school English literature class. She asks students to pause the video to complete a Stop and Jot, explaining how the image on her screen is an example of exploitation, a term that she's defined with key words underlined.

Video Clip 24: Jen Brimming

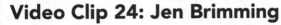

https://www.wiley.com/go/newnormal

After the pause, she displays a response. Instead of displaying the correct answer, as many teachers might do, Jen highlights a likely student answer—one that is on the right track, but doesn't quite meet her exemplar. This allows her to give targeted feedback for revision, and students to recognize the gap in their responses.

She rereads the definition of exploitation, emphasizing that the complete definition has two main parts, and gives feedback for revision. Then she adds a second idea to her first response, a clear visual reminder of the importance of revision.

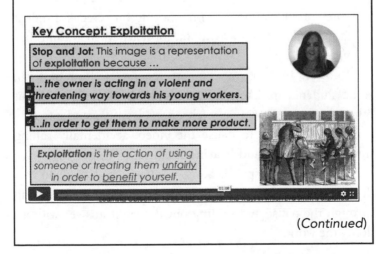

(*Continued*)

(*Continued*)

By breaking down the exemplar response into these two parts, she ensures that students who may have missed the second, subtler element can clearly see the gap in their understanding, and have the opportunity to close that gap through revision. She ends the review with an opportunity to rewrite. Revision is built into the class's structure, creating a culture of self-assessment and student accountability.

Benefits and Limitations of Implicit Assessment

When intentionally is built into the culture of the class, Implicit Assessment can help improve self-awareness and ownership of learning among students. When students are responsible for monitoring their progress, they develop independence and personal accountability for their work. If we can consistently accomplish this, it's a real win.

Implicit Assessment also maintains the pace and flow of the lesson. Further, as they are often paper and pencil activities they provide a break from working on screens. Implicit Assessment also means a lower lift for teachers in grading and individual follow-up.

However, Implicit Assessment requires a leap of faith; some students are likely to attentively check their work but others may not. During asynchronous lessons, students may miss the directions to pause the video, accidentally rolling through the pause and hearing the answer before they have had a chance to respond. Some students may even do this deliberately, learning that they can save a lot of effort by rolling through the pause and finding out the right answer without doing the work.

Beyond whether or not students do the work, what they get out of implicit assessment tasks can be an even bigger question. Some students compete tasks but still not learn much from them. This, cognitive scientists tell us, is because novices don't perceive the difference between a flawed answer and an exemplar in the same way that experts do.

According to the Dunning-Kruger Effect, the less you know about something, the less aware you are of the quality of your work. So the downside of saying, "If your answer sounded something like this, you got the point," is that students whose answers were nothing like yours might, in good faith, think, *Yeah, that's about what I said*, and neither they nor you would know the difference. In using Implicit Assessment, we must realize that many students who believe that they've answered correctly won't actually have done so, and they may not be able to revise their work accurately.

Tips for Successful Implementation

- Preface the pause with a reminder about purpose; be explicit about how each task will be used later in the lesson.

- In an asynchronous video, try keeping the video rolling through the allotted work time instead of asking students to pause. This increases the likelihood students will complete the task. Show a timer counting down, or narrate time stamps ("It's been one minute, now you have 90 seconds left.") to mark progress. In Kim Griffith's Retrieval Practice, for example, a circle gradually fills, helping students see and track their remaining time:

(Continued)

(Continued)

Retrieval Practice

1. Karl _____ published the _____ _____ which instructed the _____ to overthrow the _____.

2. Who on Manor Farm might be considered part of the bourgeoisie?

3. Name one key difference between capitalism and communism.

4. The three branches of the _____ triangle are ethos, _____ and pathos.

5. Name two key characteristics of a fable.

Teach Like a CHAMPION®
Uncommon Schools

- Provide opportunities to revise after revealing exemplar thinking. To "close the loop" on Implicit Assessment, students need to take the time to compare their responses to an exemplar and make changes accordingly.

- Be thoughtful about how you review answers so students can most accurately check their own work. For instance, you may give a visible task ("Put a check mark next to each of the following terms you included") or explain a range of correct answers.

- Be transparent about anticipated errors. Review possible mistakes while normalizing error and encouraging students in their thinking.

LAGGING ASSESSMENT

Lagging Assessment refers to moments in the lesson when students are asked to complete and submit work that teachers will later evaluate. This can allow teachers to Check for Understanding during more substantive assignments, as well as help with a lesson's Pacing. We see this in both synchronous and asynchronous lessons. In fact, the vast majority of the lessons we've watched include some form of Lagging Assessment—assessment where students receive feedback and teachers see where students are in their thinking after some delay.

In Sara Sherr's AP Literature class at Uncommon Preparatory High School in Brooklyn, Sara asks students to pause the video and take six minutes to type out their responses. She gives clear expectations for what the response should include ("an argument, a piece of evidence, and a Zoom out"). The directions, as well as a few options for what students should do if they get stuck, appear on the screen:

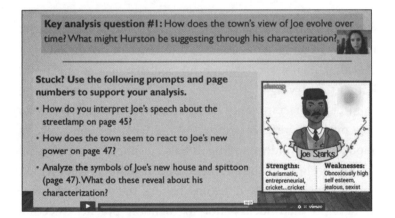

Since she can't be in the room with them, Sara has anticipated what aspects of the question students may struggle with and provided guidance and resources. After students press play again, she reminds them, "This question needs to be submitted to the Google Classroom by 2 p.m.," giving clear accountability and parameters for submission. After she receives their work, Sara will review the responses and use them to inform later lessons.

Video Clip 25: Sara Sherr
https://www.wiley.com/go/newnormal

Lagging Assessment can also allow us to collect a larger snapshot of data from all of our students. A teacher implementing Retrieval Practice, for example, may ask students to send a photo of the work they completed in their notebooks in a given time. Based on a review of this work, the teacher can then decide whether or where to prioritize additional review.

Benefits and Limitations of Lagging Assessment

Because Lagging Assessment is the most thorough form of checking, it allows for thoughtful feedback on rigorous tasks. Rather than trying to get a quick snapshot of student thinking from chats or comments, Lagging Assessment allows us to take our time, read carefully, and see what the work reveals about student understanding. It's also a simpler technological lift for teachers in the moment, and it helps protect lesson Pacing. For students, it means having the time and space to develop their ideas—not to mention practice meeting deadlines and managing their own workloads.

However, the sheer volume of content that submissions can create requires teachers to have strong systems for organizing and responding to student work. Rather than quickly tracking data over students' shoulders during class, we may now suddenly be juggling 30 emailed submissions or a ballooning Google Classroom. Teachers must think carefully about what they can realistically review and give feedback on. This may also be an area to leverage additional teaching staff or teacher support if it is available.

For all of its benefit in allowing us to get a clear read on student understanding, sometimes the lag means revealing errors and misunderstandings too late. While reviewing end-of-class assessments like Exit Tickets, for example, you may realize that a significant portion of your class misunderstood something critical to the lesson. This is a particular challenge of asynchronous lessons. It may not be until you review responses after the lesson that you realize many students struggled with something you had not anticipated.

Tips for Successful Implementation

- Use an exemplar to provide streamlined feedback.
- Preplan your systems of follow-up if a student doesn't submit work.
- Less is more: assign the work carefully so that students are more likely to complete it diligently (and we are more likely to give thoughtful feedback).
- "Dissolve the Screen" by connecting subsequent classes to your feedback ("Many of us were struggling with embedding evidence, so that'll be

(Continued)

(*Continued*)

the focus of our lesson today") or by shouting out exemplar work from prior classes.

- Include supports and/or guidance for students, as we saw in Sara Sherr's PowerPoint.

REAL-TIME ASSESSMENT

In a synchronous lesson, Real-Time Assessment refers to opportunities for teachers to check student understanding in the moment, gathering data immediately on what students are (or aren't) struggling with. It's the type of assessment that most closely mirrors checking for understanding in a brick-and-mortar classroom; since students are with us, at the same time, and in the same "place," we can assess understanding and respond immediately.

A strong example of this appears in Eric Snider's fifth-grade ELA class in Cranston Island. After students listen to an excerpt from *One Crazy Summer* by Rita Williams-Garcia, Eric tells them to pause for a "quick check." Students are asked to respond to a multiple-choice question about the excerpt, highlight evidence to support their thinking, and chat their response to Eric. He gives students one minute, and warmly thanks each as their chats roll in.

Video Clip: Eric Snider, "Delphine feels proud"

https://www.wiley.com/go/newnormal

This real-time data reveals a misconception that Eric immediately makes transparent, saying, "Before we share out number one, we're actually split, and we might be a little confused about how Delphine feels." He does not move forward, opting instead to reread a key sentence and address the misunderstanding immediately. After rereading—and before revealing the error or the correct answer—he asks students to resubmit their responses. He then says, "We're up to probably 70 percent of us have this correct, but there's still a little bit of confusion. Rather than a Cold Call, because this has been challenging, I'll actually take hands. Can someone explain to us, what's the best answer to number one and why?" Eric calls on a student (likely a student he knows has submitted the correct answer), who clearly explains the best choice, and the class moves on to the next question, gap in comprehension closed.

In a lesson from Libertas College Prep in Los Angeles, fifth-grade teacher Arrianna Chopp is teaching a synchronous lesson on the novel *Esperanza Rising*. She asks students to recall a previous lesson, take one minute, and respond to her question in the comments of the Google Classroom. As students work, she narrates the names of students who have already submitted and thanks them for their participation, occasionally giving feedback to individual students aloud ("Caleb, can you be more specific?"). Then, to start the discussion, she Cold Calls Caleb to read his response, then asks another student to add on. The accuracy of responses informs Arrianna that she can move on, so she tells the class, "I'm really loving these responses that I'm seeing. We are jumping straight into our reading." Since her Real-Time Assessment reveals that students were successful, she knows she doesn't need to spend any more time on that question and can proceed to the next section of the lesson.

Video Clip: Arrianna Chopp, "Las Ciruelas"

https://www.wiley.com/go/newnormal

Benefits and Limitations of Real-Time Assessment

Because Real-Time Assessment most closely mirrors the classroom, it can help ensure attention, engagement, and follow-through. Teachers are able to watch students working and support them in their responses, recognizing misconceptions immediately, as Eric does, and adapting lessons to address error without delay. Students feel "seen" and recognized as teachers narrate their habits or thank them for their responses. Real-Time Assessment is an opportunity not only for collecting data but also for connecting with students by acknowledging their presence, their effort, and the work that they are doing.

However, Real-Time Assessment can slow down the Pacing of lessons; taking the time for all students to chat their responses or enter into a Google Document is a real time investment. It can also be logistically challenging and is vulnerable to technological issues. Teachers must navigate platforms quickly and seamlessly to maintain the flow of the lesson, and it may be challenging to gather data in the moment. Responses also tend to be more surface level; as one teacher put it, "It's difficult to get high Think Ratio with independent tasks done in short bursts."

Tips for Successful Implementation

- Be thoughtful about your Means of Participation.

- Incorporate well-designed multiple-choice questions into your lesson. Sometimes, we avoid using MC questions because they feel less rigorous, but well-designed MC questions, as Eric demonstrates, are excellent for real-time CFU, as long as they've been carefully planned and designed.

- Leverage additional teacher support if possible. Use a co-teacher to help with tech or manage the chat.

- Incorporate revision tasks or layers of Real-Time Assessment to deepen student thinking. ("Take one of your classmates' ideas and expand it in your rewrite.")

- Consider incorporating whiteboards for math or science classes—classes with the need to produce work that's challenging to type. You might ask students to draw a diagram or solve a problem on their whiteboards and hold it up to the screen to Check for Understanding in the moment.

- In early elementary school classes, where typing into a chat or a document may be a challenge, you may opt to poll the class, using thumbs up/thumbs down or showing numbers on fingers. You might also have students hold their papers up to the screen or point to a place in their books.

IMPLICATIONS FOR PLANNING AND PRACTICE

To maximize the benefits and minimize the limitations of the three forms of assessment, teachers must carefully plan how and when to use each.

As with any lesson, they must Plan for Error—anticipate student misunderstandings and prepare responses in advance. The first step is to prioritize questions. Which questions in the lesson are highest leverage? Which are students most likely to struggle with? How do the questions build to your objective or key understanding for the day? After drafting target responses, identify likely errors. What are students likely to struggle with? What aspects of the target response are likely to be missing or incomplete? Once you have a clear sense of both the goal for the lesson and likely areas of confusion, you can plan your assessment loops. This way, you're more likely to get the data you need to accurately recognize and address anticipated misunderstandings.

As you plan your assessment loops, consider the following questions:

- How much time will students need to complete this task? How much time will you need to review responses?

- What type of feedback do you want to provide? What do you want students to do with your feedback?

- Would a misunderstanding in this moment prevent students from continuing in the lesson, or is it likely to be addressed by another question or discussion?

- Where are students in the course of the lesson or in the development of an idea? Is this early in the lesson, a place you want students to explore and experiment with ideas?

Or is this a moment when you want to see a more polished version of what students think and have taken away from the conversation?

One important piece of planning is to maximize synergy in a given lesson. For example, imagine you are teaching a synchronous lesson on Chapter 2 of Lois Lowry's *The Giver*. You may choose to give students an annotation task during their initial reading: "As we read, annotate any evidence of the ritual Jonas's family performs and jot a note to yourself about what its purpose might be." Perhaps you chose Implicit Assessment to Check for Understanding here because you know students are likely to be successful and you don't want to spend too much time reviewing their annotations. You also know that a quick review of the exemplar response will ensure students have established meaning on this section of text and are ready to move forward. After reading and giving students time to write, you might say something like, "Compare your annotation to mine. I noticed that the ritual seems to be one where all members of the family share their strongest feelings from the day and sympathize with one another. Take 20 seconds now and add the word 'sympathize' to your response."

In the same lesson, after reading several more pages, you might shift into a Real-Time Assessment loop with a chat brainstorm: "What do you notice about this ritual? Why might the family perform it? Chat your response to just me and I'll Cold Call someone to respond." At this point in the lesson, you may have chosen Real-Time Assessment because it's important for you to have a sense of where the class is as a whole — are we all on the same page? Is anyone lost? Has anyone missed an essential idea? This is still a place for students to be midstream in their thinking, so a quick response can give you the data you need to spot and address any confusion before continuing. After seeing student responses and noting trends, you could Cold Call one student to elaborate on his or her thinking, then give all students an opportunity to revise their responses.

At the end of the lesson, you may wish to close with a Lagging Assessment loop, asking students to write a longer response and answer these questions with evidence: "How would you describe this family ritual? What purpose does it seem to serve? What might this suggest about the community?" This is a question you want students to take their time on, reviewing their work from the whole lesson, and thinking about the novel more holistically. The next day's class may begin with a Show Call of exemplar work from this final write, closing the assessment loop and potentially launching into a new one, real time.

We see an example of this synergy in Ben Esser's sixth-grade class in Brooklyn. Ben and his students are reading *Chains*, by Laurie Halse Anderson. He begins his synchronous class by shouting out all students with 100% scores on their classwork. Then he says, "Everybody, there was one trend about a spot where people were confused . . . let me point out where the misunderstanding happened." He notes that "people really nailed it" on one aspect of the question, but "people really struggled" with understanding another character's perspective.

 ## Video Clip: Ben Esser, "Misunderstanding"

https://www.wiley.com/go/newnormal

This is an example of Lagging Assessment—students answered questions at the end of the prior day's lesson, Ben reviewed them after class, and he saw this trending gap in comprehension. From that insight, he then names the error he saw, clearly stamps that this was incorrect, and rereads the question with some additional framing to address the confusion. He says, "Don't answer in the chat. You're actually going to go revise yesterday's Exit Ticket, by answering that question in today's classwork... you have two minutes to write out your answer."

By following up on the prior day's Lagging Assessment with Real-Time Assessment in class, Ben both ensures student mastery of the objective and continues to build a culture where student ideas are valued and understanding is the top priority.

Note that these are just a few examples of synergies among assessment loops. The ones you choose to use—and the way you choose to use them—will vary based on your goals in the moment and the needs of your students at a given time.

Two Favorite TLAC Techniques for Online CFU

- Cold Call, the act of calling on students who have not raised their hands, has always been a favorite technique of ours. Teachers can use Cold Call to send the message that everyone's thinking is important, not just those who volunteer. Cold Call is also a form of Real-Time Assessment; it's an opportunity to check one student's understanding

  (Continued)

(Continued)

in order to gauge more widespread misunderstanding. You may call on someone whose answer you already know, or use it as a "blind" temperature for the rest of the room. In order for Cold Call to be an effective means of checking for understanding, students must feel comfortable making mistakes and learning from them with their peers.

- Show Call, a type of Cold Call that involves taking students' written work and displaying it to the class, is a flexible technique that can be used in conjunction with several forms of assessment. You may opt to use Show Call as a follow-up to Lagging Assessment, closing a gap or addressing a misunderstanding about something that has been submitted previously. In an asynchronous lesson, Show Call can become an opportunity for Implicit Assessment as students note differences between their own and the student example; in a synchronous lesson, you may choose to incorporate Real-Time Assessment, if students respond to the work directly, revising their work in the moment to address some element of the exemplar.

We've realized that there are few hard-and-fast rules when it comes to using assessment loops to Check for Understanding; the process by which teachers plan and prepare is much more important. There will always be a variety of worthy pathways toward mastery, so teachers must decide, based on their lesson, the misunderstandings they anticipate, and their knowledge of their students, which is most valuable in a given moment.

Crucially, checking for understanding is one of the primary drivers of relationship building in classrooms: through CFU, teachers communicate to students that their success is important, their ideas matter, and their teachers believe in them. The importance of this message is compounded online. Without the warm, genuine classroom interactions we all miss, CFU loops allow us to Dissolve the Screen and show students that we see them, and that we still value their thinking, their success, and their learning.

ASSESSMENT LOOPS AND CHECKING FOR UNDERSTANDING: IN REVIEW

Assessment Loops are a way for teachers to collect data and monitor student understanding, and for students to consolidate understanding and develop self-assessment skills. They also help create a culture of collective accountability.

- **Implicit Assessment:** Implicit Assessment involves students checking their own work against a model. And while Implicit Assessment can help grow self-awareness and ownership of learning among students, it takes a leap of faith. Students may not do the work, or do the work without getting much out of it.

- **Lagging Assessment:** Lagging Assessment asks students to complete and submit work to be later evaluated. While it can allow teachers to Check for Understanding during more substantive assignments, as well as help with a lesson's Pacing, the lag can mean missing out on misunderstanding in the moment.

- **Real-Time Assessment:** Real-Time Assessment most closely mirrors the classroom. While it can help ensure attention, engagement, and follow-through, it can also slow down lesson Pacing—not to mention being logistically challenging and vulnerable to technological issues.

- **Implications for Planning and Practice.** To best leverage synergies among the three forms of assessment, planning is hugely important. Your plan will ultimately rest on your goals in the moment and the needs of your students at a given time.

Chapter 6

Procedures and Routines

Darryl Williams and Dan Cotton

In the classroom, procedures and routines are the key to ensuring student focus and attention. Having a right way to do familiar tasks allows you to move smoothly from activity to activity, keeping the thread of instruction alive. This keeps students engaged. But the power of consistent, familiar procedures is doubled when we teach online, the lines between school and life are blurrier than they have ever been, and students may participate while sitting at the kitchen table, slumped on a couch, or lying on the floor of their bedroom. A predictable daily schedule, clarity about materials required, and familiar and visible ways for students to participate all benefit parents, too, enabling them to more easily help their students be successful while navigating demands on their own time and attention—nontrivial demands such as caring for family members, and quite possibly working from home.

One of the benefits of strong procedures is that, once a procedure has been internalized by students, it can be launched with a concise cue—for example, "Enter your thoughts in the chat. Go!" When that happens the continuity of instruction and the flow of ideas are preserved. The lesson moves along with energy and purpose. It's a better class for everyone.

That's why we love this video of Spanish teacher Knikki Hernandez from William Monroe High School in Stanardsville, Virginia. Her clear procedures help ensure that her class flows, and that her students are prepared, attentive, and actively engaged.

 Video Clip: Knikki Hernandez, "Cuaderno"

https://www.wiley.com/go/newnormal

Knikki opens her lesson with a "materials slide" describing what students need to have with them to be successful at the start of class. Taking a minute to make sure everyone has the right materials and expectations gets everyone ready to learn, and you can see that in the video. When Knikki puts up her materials slide, one of her students jumps up to get *un lapiz* (a pencil). She hadn't realized she'd be expected to write.

But the really powerful procedures become visible once Knikki starts teaching. She uses Cold Call right away. In an online world, Cold Call is powerful, maybe even essential. Distraction is a click away, students are hesitant to volunteer and we're trying to connect through a tiny keyhole in the bottom of the screen. Involving students regularly and unpredictably keeps them attentive, normalizes participation and makes students feel seen and important.

Knikki uses Cold Call three times in the clip, each in a different way:

> First, she uses it to signal her expectation for active engagement: "Abby, what does this question say— *Que necesito para la clase hoy?*" she asks one student. By Cold Calling as soon as class starts, Knikki signals its normalcy. She's letting students know they should be prepared to speak and to be engaged and active. And her student, in fact, *smiles when she's Cold Called.* Perhaps she feels seen by her teacher, important. She's fine with the Cold Call. She gets the message: Be ready. You'll be an active learner in Spanish, and she's quick to adapt.

> Next, Knikki uses Cold Call to check students' understanding of the independent task just before they begin. She asks one student invitingly, "What are we doing for the next three minutes and 11 seconds? Where are we writing our definitions?" Three minutes and 11 seconds is a lot of time to waste if you are unsure of the task. Again, Knikki knows that if she asks for a volunteer, those who are unclear will likely hide. This way she gets a much better read on whether students understand the task.

With the directions now clearly understood, students immediately jump into work. Knikki gives them three minutes to work independently. At this point, there's been enough Cold Calling that students probably suspect that Knikki will use it to ask some of them to share their work, so the incentive is to work hard. And, surprise! That's exactly what she does: warmly and engagingly Cold Calling. After the timer goes off,

Knikki begins (in Spanish), "Ok guys, let's continue with the vocabulary and let's start with Raquel. What do you have for patient?"

We call this "backstopping" independent work by following it with Cold Calls. It makes sure students complete the work, allows you to review their answers more quickly, and to assessing everyone's level of understanding, not just volunteers. With the backstop to make sure it's effective, Knikki is able to use a super-simple, low-tech activity already familiar to students, knowing it will be productive.

Cold Call is a simple procedure, but it has profound effects that cascade through the culture of the session.

MEANS OF PARTICIPATION

What we call Means of Participation are all the ways students can participate in class, especially when the procedures are made transparent—when students know how and when to use them. In a brick-and-mortar classroom, Means of Participation are typically Turn and Talk, Everybody Writes, Cold Call, and Volunteers (the teacher calling on students who've raised their hands). Online, the spirit is the same, but the means themselves are slightly different. The primary Means of Participation in a synchronous lesson are:

- Breakout Rooms
- Cold Call
- Volunteers
- "Chat"
- Everybody Writes

The key for any of these is having a consistent routine. Take Breakout Rooms, for example. Breakout Rooms can be incredibly productive, allowing lots of students to talk through an idea, hear a peer's insights, and have a moment to rehearse or refine their thinking in a low-risk setting before sharing with the whole group. But the challenges are greater online. In a classroom, you can manage a room of small-group discussions or Turn and Talks with relative ease, making sure peer-to-peer conversations are productive, on-task, and not consistently dominated by some students. Online, you can't simply glance out across all the Breakout Rooms and assess the degree of engagement. With that in mind, here are a few notes on using the basic Means of Participation in online classrooms:

- **Breakout Rooms**. We like to err on the side of small rooms (two or three) and find that it's often helpful to vary group size slightly. If group size is more than two, we sometimes set ground rules to make sure everyone is encouraged and allowed to speak: "The person whose first name comes first in the alphabet should kick off the conversation." A reminder of the backstopping Cold Call ("When we come back, I'll choose a few of you to share your thoughts") or even a precall ("When we come back I'll ask Jillian and then Lizzette to start us off") is often helpful.

  You'll want to explain a clear procedure for Breakout Rooms too, so students know what they should look like. Something like: "When you get to your Breakout Room greet your partner very quickly but then ask them what they thought so you are sure to be talking about the question within a few seconds." If the breakouts involve activities more complex than just a discussion (quizzing one another in math facts or Spanish vocabulary) you might even show them a quick video where you and another teacher model what their work in the Breakout Room should look like.

And look for a few more tech-y suggestions on Breakout Rooms in the next chapter.

- **Cold Call.** Explain to students that you'll be using it and why ("It's important for me to hear from all of you; even sometimes when you're not sure you're ready to share"). Be warm and inclusive in your tone: asking someone what they think is a good thing. We also love "pair calling" or "group calling," as in "Great, Chloe and Rodrigo, you guys were a pair. Would one of you share the solutions you came up with?"

- **Volunteering**. This can involve calling on hand raisers or allowing an "open floor" for anyone who'd like to speak. The benefits of hand raising are that it allows for more Wait Time, and you can distribute opportunities more broadly to class members. But you must be specific about requirements—about whether students physically raise their hands or to use an electronic "raise hand" function. Each has its challenges. It's easy to miss raised hands because not everyone is on your screen, but it can be just as hard to toggle to the participants list to see who's raised an electronic hand. We often like to let students raise their hand "on screen" like they do in class—it's less screen toggling for them and we can often read something about their affect in how they raise their hand—but this means we have to rotate which students we see first on the screen during the lesson to make sure to balance those we are most likely to call on. But we also find we can go open floor more easily—and that participation is more energetic and equitable—when we Cold Call early on.

- **"Chat."** The "chat" function is one of our favorite tools. Most frequently we see teachers use it as a formative thinking exercise. "Please enter a short response describing the mood of the chapter in the chat." This causes everyone to answer the question and engage. It also allows everyone to see what everyone else is thinking. And it lets you adapt your lessons to your students. Your next question might be, "Tell me more about why you said 'gloomy,' Kevin," or "Do any of your classmates' responses surprise you, Keshia?" Remember, too, that you can have students chat their answers to just you instead of "everybody." Then you can honor some of the most thought-provoking answers by sharing them. "Great. Here are a couple of the really interesting ideas you sent me."

- **Everybody Writes (sometimes via a Google Doc or Similar).** "Everybody Writes" describes participation tools where students write first and often are encouraged to think in writing—that is to develop ideas that are not yet formal or correct. For example, we love letting students "Stop and Jot" with paper and pencil before they are asked to participate more publicly. The jotting feels familiar to them and it's low stakes (i.e., it's clearly "just for them" and no one else will see it). But we find it pairs well with the chat or even a round of questioning. First, students Stop and Jot in a notebook, then we say, "Great. Please share one of your thoughts in the chat" or "Tell us what you wrote about, Andrew."

  Allowing students to see and respond to one another's ideas in writing so they can develop their thinking as a group is another key part of Everybody Writes, and it's especially important online, when students are as isolated from each other as they are from you. Working together in a shared Google doc can help students practice these important skills in a remote setting. We'll only mention this briefly, here, as we'll cover useful tech tools in Chapter 7.

Beyond the basics, there are variations. Watch this scene from Ben Esser's lesson, for example.

Video Clip: Ben Esser, "Wait question"
https://www.wiley.com/go/newnormal

Ben wants to make two procedures clear: "Speed Questions" and "Wait Questions." He explains what each means for students. "If I say it's a speed question, your goal is to be the first one to answer it.... If I say it's a Wait Question, I want you to wait until I say go before you press enter."

In one case he wants students to chime in with their thoughts as they have them. He wants to keep things moving and ensure an active and dynamic feeling. In the other, he wants students to take their time and think without the influence of their peers' ideas or the pressure to be fast.

Later, Ben introduces "Verbal Answers," a procedure where students raise a hand via Zoom and unmute themselves when called on to speak. Having a system of specific, individual procedures for how students respond to different types of questions puts Ben in a good position to engineer student participation, steer lesson Pacing, and adapt his questioning in response to student work.

You can also see that Ben has done his homework. His questions are planned in advance and posted for students to see on his PowerPoint slide. Ben labels each question

"Wait Questions," "Speed Questions," or "Verbal Answers." This makes it easier for students to respond accordingly. Ben wants students to build the habit of how to respond to each type of question. More than labeling, before asking each question, Ben reminds students what type of question it is. His coupling of visual cues with verbal reminders helps avoid any ambiguity or confusion for students. And because of Ben's attentiveness to this critical academic system, students beautifully follow through, responding to each question type as he expects.

Ben succeeds in avoiding some of the problems that can occur when teachers are unclear in explaining their Means of Participation: the problem of crickets, and imbalanced voice equity?

Crickets are those questions that no one seems to want to answer. Cold Call both solves that problem and normalizes participating. We often find in our workshops that a few Cold Calls erodes any reluctance among participants, and once-reticent groups are soon full of volunteers. Writing also can solve the crickets problem. It's a little safer to weigh in in writing, especially when everyone else is also doing it.

On the other side of the coin, having clear procedures for participation also helps you ensure "voice equity," the right of everyone—not just the quick, vociferous and highly verbal—to speak and be heard. When a few students monopolize the discussion by always going first, some of our students—typically our most vulnerable—can get left out of critical learning opportunities.

Ben emphasizes the idea of voice equity when he explains the expectations for responding to "Wait Questions: "The idea here is we want to give everybody an opportunity to think and write. And that way if you want, you can read some of your classmates' responses after you enter your response." With his procedures in place, Ben can choose to take a hand, Cold Call, or allow a little Wait Time. He can ask everyone to chat and choose the most fruitful answers for a follow-up: "Why did you say the mood was tense, Damari?"

Not only that, but the phrase "you can read some of your classmates' responses after you enter your response" is important. It frames and clarifies habits for responding to one another respectfully and carefully (we call this Habits of Discussion in Teach Like a Champion). More than simply understanding how to respond to prompts, students are hearing guidelines for how to interact with each other.

STUDENT WORKSPACE: LAYING A FOUNDATION FOR INDEPENDENCE

Part of your classroom is someone's kitchen. Or couch. Or the hallway outside their apartment. These are the places students are now working from—sometimes by necessity, but also sometimes by choice and without much forethought. Many 13-year-olds left to their own devices would rather join class from the foot of their bed and with no good place to write. But the details of where they sit and what their workspace is like can have an impact on their ability to focus and participate. Teaching students how to set up their remote workspace is a core system and routine—one that pays long-term dividends.

Consider this moment from the first day of Matthew Diamond's asynchronous Geography class at KIPP St. Louis HS. At the outset, to teach students how to set up their workspace, Matthew presents a snapshot of his own:

His narration offers a quick tour: Pick a quiet space so you can focus. You'll need a notebook and writing utensil. Clear the space to minimize distractions. His tour provides the rationale that students, particularly in high school, crave. It says not just "Here's What to Do," but also "Here's why my expectations will help you be successful." Matthew's use of his own workspace to illustrate to his students how to set their space up has an additional benefit of dissolving the screen: We're all working from home. This is a bit of who I am.

OPENING SEQUENCE

A key way to boost students' comfort and confidence at the start of a lesson is through a consistent opening routine. By presenting to students exactly what materials they need to have at the ready, how they are expected to engage, and how the lesson will unfold, teachers can set their students up not just to be present, but to learn. Consistency here is key. With many of the regular rhythms of school disrupted, a consistent opening provides familiarity and clarity, subtly building students' confidence that they know What to Do from the outset.

For a strong example, take a look at the openings of Alonzo Hall and Linda Frazier's lessons. Both are middle school math teachers at Uncommon Schools.

Video Clip: Alonzo Hall and Linda Frazier, "Let's get organized"

https://www.wiley.com/go/newnormal

As Alonzo and Linda made the shift to asynchronous instruction, consistency and predictability were paramount. Although students had spent several months with them in their classrooms learning math content, this was an unfamiliar learning context. They need to spend some time introducing core procedures in their opening lessons.

Both Linda and Alonzo are warm and measured as they open their lesson. Neither teacher wants to rush the setup and risk confusion or uncertainty among their students. Not only do they take time to explain the procedures clearly, but they also encourage students to use the pause button to take their time and make sure they're ready. Saying "Pause to get set up if you need to," says "This is important. Take the time to do it right."

Both teachers are diligent about making important procedures clear both verbally and visually, highlighting them in yellow so students notice them. Alonzo makes this transparent: "Whenever the yellow highlight comes across our page it is simply a reminder that you can/should pause the video to copy the notes from the page." Linda reminds students of the importance of her visuals by saying, "Please pause to make your paper look like mine."

One of the hallmarks of schools with strong cultures is a consistency of expectations from room to room. Shared procedures help both students *and* teachers be more successful. The more familiar and consistent the procedures are, the more students will get used to them—and ultimately the more successful they will be. For teachers, too, rather than inventing everything on their own, shared procedures and routines mean they can focus their time and energy on adapting their content to the online system. For both teachers and students, a consistent approach says: We are still a school; we're still connected.

With online lessons, your opening sequence, or procedure for how to get started, helps establish (or strengthen) a personal connection with students and set expectations for the lesson. In many of the opening sequences we've studied, several unassuming but effective procedures for starting the lesson have emerged.

1. **Greeting:** In the same way teachers would warmly and positively greet their students at the classroom door, we've noticed teachers typically open their lessons with their face visible on the screen, offering a warm greeting, orienting students to where they are in their learning sequence, and reminding everyone that they still exist within a cohesive learning community. The unspoken message should be: "I'm happy to see you and we have great things to do together."

2. **Orientation Screen:** Many of the lessons we study post a slide with clear directions for the materials and preliminary tasks that students need to get started. Amanda Moloney's is a good example (you'll see others throughout the book). After greeting her students with her face visible in her asynchronous lesson, Amanda, who teaches Year 1s at Ballarat Clarendon College in Victoria, Australia, shifts to a slide titled, "What You Will Need." The slide is simple and easily followed, listing materials students need to engage in the lesson. To further support her students, Amanda adds an image of those materials.

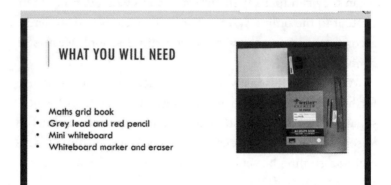

3. **Opening Task:** In a few places, we have emphasized the importance of starting quickly. Whether asynchronous or synchronous, it's critical to get students moving and interacting with the content and, if the lesson is synchronous, with one another—right away. The message should be "Expect to be actively engaged." Waiting more than a few minutes to do that can undercut that message.

The opening of Joshua Humphrey's asynchronous ninth-grade math lesson offers a case study in how to do this. After a brief (25-second) explanation of the day's objectives, Josh and his students are down to business. "First things first," Josh says and smiles. "Just like in our other class, you all have a Do Now. So this video is about to pause, and I want you to put in your answers, #1, #2, #3 . . . I'm pausing it right now." Josh's warmth Dissolves the Screen, but his Economy of Language—no extraneous words—provides students the clarity of knowing exactly What to Do. Within one minute of the opening of the lesson they are actively engaging with the content.

It's the same for synchronous lessons—you might recall how quickly Knikki Hernandez gets started. In any an online environment, it's important for students to be actively engaged right away. The longer you wait, the harder it gets—and the more passive the engagement.

WHAT TO DO: YOUR DIRECTIONS ARE PART OF THE SYSTEM

The success of an online lesson rests heavily on students' ability to follow through on directions and complete activities. They are far from their teacher, meaning follow-through is often difficult (synchronous) or impossible (asynchronous) to discern. Giving directions that are clear and concise—what we call What to Do—can be the difference between following through and not and is foundational to ensuring student success.

Observe, for example, how both Linda Frazier and Alonzo Hall rely on What to Do as part of their opening sequences. They give both verbal and visual directions and highlight them in yellow so students notice them.

One of the pitfalls Linda and Alonzo avoid is delivering directions that are unnecessarily lengthy or ambiguous.

Directives like "Make sure you're ready for today's lesson" don't explicitly tell students what they need to do to "get ready." A more effective direction might be, "For today's lesson, you'll need your novel, reading journal, and a pencil. Take 60 seconds to pause the video and get your materials now." The clearer and more precise you are, the more likely you'll get engagement and follow and the more likely students will be successful.

Notice the wonderful clarity of George Bramley's directions at Brigshaw High School in Leeds, England, during his lesson on the Battle of Hastings. When prompting students to jot notes on the Battle, George says, "Please pause this video now while you fill in that box." Because note-taking will be a recurring academic task, George has begun to assign consistent language to his directions. "Please pause the video now," "directly into the Word document," and "fill in that box" are all phrases that will become cues that help students follow through. Over time, standardizing (and tightening) the language can minimize room for misunderstanding.

Students in the lessons we've observed aren't left to figure out how to engage, even in their asynchronous lessons. In the most successful (virtual) classrooms, teachers plan the consistent language and phrasing they'll use for activities as carefully as other parts of their lesson. This helps students to be more likely to follow through, complete tasks successfully, and build habits for academic success.

TEACHER-FACING PROCEDURES

While explaining effective participation procedures clearly and building them into the fabric of your newly online teaching can be a challenge, it's not the only one. Another is maintaining working memory—and by that we mean your own limited supply of it.

Even the best plan—a quick write in the chat here to get everyone thinking; a few Cold Calls; an opportunity for volunteers/taking hands, into a Breakout Room; and another quick write—isn't very useful if you can't remember it. There's so much to think about while teaching online, it's not hard to forget when to Cold Call and when to "chat."

That's why we also want to share the benefits of consistent teacher-facing procedures—things you can do to help yourself support student-facing procedures.

Below is an example of a slide from one of our workshops. Notice how we've placed icons in the bottom right-hand corner. Each icon, as the key on the right indicates, reminds us to use different types of participation. In this example, the group icon followed by a horn reminds us that we want to give participants time to share their thoughts in a Breakout Room before we Cold Call or take a hand to commence the group discussion. Another might use the chat icon followed by a horn to say we'll ask participants to put their ideas into the chat and then Cold Call someone to kick-off the conversation. There are any number of combinations for blending participation types.

And that's what makes it so much to remember: there are so many combinations, across so many lessons, across so many days. Anything we can do to limit the amount of brain space devoted to remembering the "how" of lesson delivery stands to vastly improve its "what." With these small reminders to ourselves, we free up some portion of our working memory—a working memory that is in high demand. And if we don't have to remember, "Wait, was it supposed to be a chat or a Cold Call at this point?," we free ourselves up to do more and better.

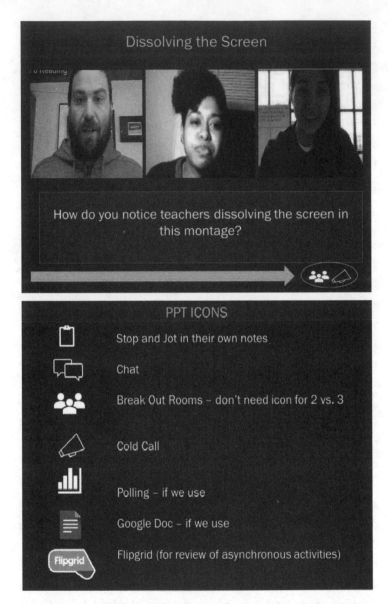

So steal our icons, or adapt them, or develop your own system. Whatever you do, make these kinds of "notes to self" a consistent part of how you plan your lessons. You can thank us later.

PROCEDURES AND ROUTINES: IN REVIEW

In any classroom, there's power in procedures—in having a right way to do familiar tasks and activities. In an online setting, some are especially important. Teachers, parents, and students all stand to benefit from their use.

- **Means of Participation:** Means of Participation are sort of standardized ways students can participate in class. When used correctly, they can improve a class's Pacing and keep students engaged. They are varied and many, and the key is being consistent with those that you use.

- **Student Workspace—Laying a Foundation for Independence:** Teaching students how to set up their remote workspace is a core system and routine—one that pays long-term dividends. Taking the time to get this right is especially important when the classroom is the kitchen or bedroom or . . . you get the idea.

- **Opening Sequence:** With many of the regular rhythms of school disrupted, a consistent opening is key to good outcomes. Just be consistent, be warm, and get on with it in the first few minutes.

- **What to Do—Your Directions Are Part of the System:** Students can't follow through if they misunderstand the directions. Especially online, it's essential to make directions as clear as possible—with as little room for ambiguity as possible.

- **Teacher-Facing Procedures:** Cognitive load is as limited a resource in teachers as it is in students. Do what you can to lessen the tax on your own cognitive load by building systems that benefit you. Give your memory a rest and your teaching will be better for it.

Chapter 7

Classroom Tech
Rob Richard and John Costello

The previous chapters in this book describe a set of tools for building strong relationships with students and improving the quality of their remote learning. With all the talk of Breakout Rooms and students responding in the chat function, though, many teachers may understandably be asking, "Okay, that sounds great, but how exactly do I do that?" While many teachers are tech savvy, others are far more comfortable molding minds with more familiar tools like pencil and paper. This has been a real part of our own experience, too. Until recently, some members of our team knew precious little about remote teaching technology. Many of the teachers we have trained have found themselves feeling anxious to try things they've only recently heard of, like Zoom, Meet and Docs. It can feel like a lot.

We want to make adapting your teaching from physical to remote classrooms as easy and seamless as possible. Learning some new tricks will be necessary, but we also think that every second you don't have to worry about how to use a new platform, or get back to the home screen, or find where the unmute icon is hiding is a moment you can spend attending to students and their educational needs.

Simplicity has been and remains our core principle. In this chapter, our goal is to provide solutions that make teaching easier—that decrease the cognitive load on teachers' working memory. We will identify simple solutions for common problems and highlight a few key details that will help bring out your best and your students'.

Before we get started, it's important to note: there's some technical guidance in this chapter, and our default is to tell you how to do it in Zoom. That said, all the basic features (chat, screen sharing, polling, and Breakout Rooms) are common across most top-tier platforms, so the tips and tools in this chapter should apply regardless of the platform your school has chosen.

Also, the help centers for most platforms like Zoom or Google Meet are excellent resources for tutorials on the tools we discuss here, and others. They usually explain using well-designed videos as opposed to the utterly incomprehensible directions you may have seen elsewhere that advise you to go to a dropdown menu that you still can't find after ten minutes of looking. While we can tell you a few things about how to apply their tools to teaching, specifically, they're better qualified to tell you how their system works. If you need to get out of the weeds, try there first.

At the end of the day, teaching online requires the same things as teaching in classrooms: the ability to explain ideas and bring them to life; the ability to engage students in learning; the ability to connect and be clear about expectations. Our primary goal is to help you use technology to adapt those familiar things to a new setting.

RECORDING YOURSELF

In March 2017, Professor Robert Kelly did a live interview on the BBC from his home office in South Korea. You might not remember his name, but we're pretty sure you've seen his video—the one where Kelly comes off as a most relatable sort of Everyman (https://www.youtube.com/watch?v=Mh4f9AYRCZY).

He was working from home, but clearly carefully prepared for his time on television. Kelly is a political scientist, and the map on the wall and the shelves of books are carefully curated to communicate knowledge and expertise. He wore a suit and tie. He had good lighting. But as he shared his thoughts on the ouster of South Korean President Park Geun-hye, his four-year-old daughter made a grand entrance in the background. As the live interview rolled, she bounced happily into the room with a jaunty walk, directly behind her unsuspecting father, closely followed by her baby brother in a walker, and then, soon after, by his clearly mortified wife, who frantically attempted to pull the children out of the room. The video became an internet sensation. During the interruption, Kelly never lost his composure. Asked about the incident later, Kelly noted that he just kept on talking about the topic at hand because "the show must go on."

It's quite possible, if you've been teaching online from your kitchen or office or living room, that you've had your own

Robert Kelly moments. Perhaps you've tried to teach with your own four-year-old bursting into the room, or when the plumber suddenly arrived, or a fire alarm went off.

Even though you know that "the show must go on," you also know that recording your lessons from home has some challenges that the classroom doesn't. Even so, it's important that we rise to meet them. If students can't clearly see you or your chart paper, they will start to tune out. If you're constantly interrupted or drowned out by competing sounds, your students will become more easily distracted. Remember, your students are also home with their families in houses and apartments full of sounds and interruptions. You might not be able to get the background or Hollywood-quality lighting, but there a few basic keys to a successful recording:

- **Background:** A neutral background works best. Find a blank wall or an interior without anything too distracting.

- **Clothing:** As much as possible, dress as you would in the classroom. This will signal that what we're doing is still school. Wear clothing that contrasts with your background so you're easy to see and that doesn't distract.

- **Lighting:** A light source in front of you will be most effective. Natural light from a window is often more soothing to viewers than light from a lamp, but try not to sit with your back to a bright window or significant light source because it can wash out your face, and you want your students to clearly see your expressions and smiles.

- **Sound:** As much as possible, eliminate background noises. Record your lessons when things are likely to be quiet. Consider using a headset to record because this generally brings the microphone closer to your mouth.

Tool Tips: Recording Yourself

- Tracking: When you're sharing an image, document, or PowerPoint on the screen, let students know where they should focus their attention. Help direct students by indicating where on the screen they should be looking, just as you would in your classroom: "We're here, starting the second paragraph now." Using animations on PowerPoint can be a great tool to show students where to focus their attention. This image from Joshua Humphrey's lesson is a great example. As he discusses each point, a tiny circle focuses student attention on the key detail.

- Camera position: We know it can be difficult to find the ideal place to record your lesson. That said, if your computer's camera is level with your face, you'll avoid the appearance of looking awkwardly downward throughout the lesson. It will also make it easier to capture the full range of natural facial expressions. If you're having trouble, try propping your laptop up on a book or two, or consider investing in a laptop stand.

- **Monitor Yourself:** Most recording programs have a window where you can see yourself as you're being filmed. Use this monitor to make sure that timers, books, and whiteboard aren't being mirror-reflected (you don't want them to read backward in the final video). When you model raising your hand, raise your palm to the camera instead of raising it over your head and out of the frame.

- **Picture in Picture:** When displaying lesson materials, set your screen so students can see your face as well your lesson materials. This is done automatically when you record in Zoom, but you can increase the range of your options by using the "screen recording" feature in PowerPoint or a basic Screencast app. This image from Chloe Hykin's lesson shows how she's placed her face in the middle of her lesson materials. This means following along for students requires less eye movement and allows her to direct students' gaze.

(Continued)

(Continued)

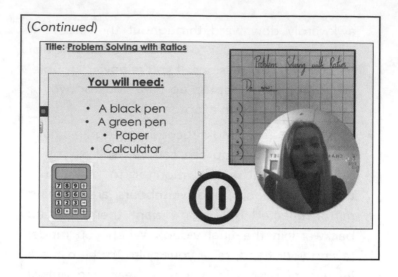

Whether you are teaching a synchronous or asynchronous lesson, these tips will minimize distractions and help keep students focused on you and your lesson. Even when you're teaching synchronously, we recommend recording your lessons anyway. Having a record of your lessons is useful for absent students and also a valuable tool for coaching and self-study.

CHAT

In one of our recent meetings, we saw a high school teacher facilitating a reading discussion. After giving students 30 seconds to organize their notes, she said, "Now go into the chat and tell me two character flaws you noticed in this chapter of *Othello*." The chat box quickly filled up with student responses. The teacher scanned the comments as they rolled in: "Great examples, Kim. Kaymesha said that Roderigo is gullible . . . love that." The teacher heard from the whole group in roughly a minute, and the students got to see everyone's responses. And importantly, *all* students engaged in sharing out.

Though the chat feature should not be the only form of participation, it can increase engagement by allowing more students to interact with the lesson at once. Arguably, there are even some advantages to using chat over regular classroom discussion:

- When students all put their responses in the chat, you can Check for Understanding with the whole class.

- You can also privately check in with a single student. No need for the illusion of privacy. Other students truly can't tell when you're having a private conversation.

- You can use the chat to prime the pump for discussion at a later time. Have the whole class generate evidence-based predictions, then turn back to those verbatim responses at a key moment in the lesson.

Tool Tips: Chat

- Review Chats Later: You can download a history of the chats in your lesson if you want to review them later. In fact, you can set up Zoom to automatically record the chat history of each lesson. They will be sorted by date in the Zoom folder within your My Documents folder.

- Get Help When You Can: If possible, have a co-teacher who can help monitor the chat. Some schools have one lead teacher delivering the lesson while other teachers can manage individual

(*Continued*)

(Continued)

students using the "private message" feature in the chat.

- **Show Call:** Screenshot or copy and paste the chat responses into a document so you can Show Call it later.

- **Direct to Teacher:** Asking students to chat so everyone can read their thoughts is a great way to build formative thinking. But sometimes you might want to slow things down a bit. Maybe you want to lower the stakes, perhaps choose a few answers that are most useful, or even share anonymous thoughts as with a Show Call. In those cases, you can mix it up by saying: "This time, chat your answer directly to me instead of everybody."

- **Outbound Chat:** You can use the chat to send key information to students—say, the link to a Google Doc they need or the question you want them to discuss in Breakout Rooms or independent work time.

BREAKOUT ROOMS

A bit more advanced than Chat, "Breakout Rooms" is a feature that allows a meeting facilitator to split the larger group into separate "rooms." A facilitator can choose to create rooms automatically or manually, and the facilitator can "drop in" on the rooms at any time. (Most platforms have tutorials on how to use this feature. Zoom is no exception.)

Specifically, Breakout Rooms are a great way for teachers to bring Turn and Talk to their online classrooms. Many of the keys to an effective Turn and Talk in the classroom are also important to its success online. There are two sets of tools successful teachers use both in the classroom and online. The first set includes tools teachers almost always use to maximize efficiency and accountability:

- **Standardized In-Cue and Out-Cue:** Use a concise phrase to prompt students in and out of the Turn and Talk. A clear starting cue launches the Turn and Talk with energy. A standardized cue is one that you use *every* time. A standardized cue increases efficiency because students automatically know what it means and What to Do.

- **Precise Time Limits:** Use specific time increments to show that time allocation is intentional. In Breakout Rooms, one- to three-minute discussions are often the sweet spot. You can use the Broadcast feature to remind students how much time they have left: "You have 30 seconds left to share." Breakout Rooms also allow you to have participants automatically return to the main session after a preset time (15 seconds, 30 seconds, 60 seconds). Use this feature to give students time to wrap up their discussions and prepare to return to the main session, but keep it consistent so they get used to the system. ("Oh, I have 30 seconds left, that's enough time to share one last thought.")

- **Crest of the Wave:** Time your breakouts so the partner discussion ends at the crest of energy, not as it peters out. Students should still be eager to participate when they get back. You can check the crest by joining one or two of the Breakout Rooms to assess whether conversations are continuing to build or if they've naturally started to subside.

Breakout Rooms are a great way to check in on the class in smaller groups. In this example, Achievement First teacher Ben Esser drops in on one of the Breakout Rooms in his class. He joins students conversation, offers feedback, and then moves on to another Breakout Room—not unlike the way he'd walk the rows in his classroom.

Video Clip: Ben Esser, "Misunder-standing"

https://www.wiley.com/go/newnormal

You can choose to end conversations early by closing the Breakout Rooms, or add additional time by messaging students with the "broadcast to all" feature. In our online training sessions, our colleague Rob will often message participants with a reminder like, "You have 30 more seconds to continue sharing."

The second set of tools that you can *sometimes* use include:

- **Managed Turns:** It's helpful sometimes to designate who starts a conversation. This gets things going faster—fewer preliminaries—and makes sure that some students don't always dominate their pairs. You might try, "The person who's first name comes first alphabetically should start when you get to your rooms." If turn-taking is important, you can use the message function to cue groups to switch. Halfway through a breakout you could message: "Student two should now be sharing."

- **Wrap with Cold Call:** Use Cold Call coming out of Breakout Rooms to hold students accountable for meaningful, on-topic conversation. Teachers can make this explicit heading into the Turn and Talk ("and coming out, I'll Cold

Call") so that it's predictable and positive, not a gotcha. Wrapping with Cold Call also sustains pace and energy. It may also be helpful to precall students in the Breakout Rooms: "When we come back, I'll ask Asha to start us off."

- **Written Task:** Have each student Stop and Jot some initial thoughts using pencil and paper to prepare for going to Breakout Rooms. This has three benefits: (1) it ensures both students have something to say, (2) it makes it more likely that both will speak, and (3) it supports students in listening to their partner because they don't have to keep their idea in their heads.

- **Partner Share:** Have students share out what their partner said after a breakout to increase accountability for listening and to support processing of their peers' ideas.

Tool Tips: Breakout Rooms

- Broadcasting: Take advantage of the "Broadcast to All" feature in Breakout Rooms to communicate with students in a noninvasive way. If you've given your students a prompt to discuss, broadcast the written prompt so students have it handy. Let them know how much time they have left, or remind them when another student should begin talking.

- Dropping In: As with Turn and Talk, it's nice to drop into a group's discussion and check in with their thinking. For younger students, and at the beginning of the year, it's helpful to drop in more

(Continued)

(Continued)

often for shorter periods of time. Once students become accustomed to the system and can reliably work in small groups, you can spend longer periods of time picking out bright spots and supporting struggling students. Ben Esser's video from earlier in this chapter is a great example of how to do that.

- **Breakout Group Size:** Keep them small; no more than two or three students in each room is our most common size. Re-create the rooms regularly, varying which students are paired together. Remember, the more students you add to a group, the less time students have to participate—and the more likely they are to meander off-task.

- **Breakout Group Composition:** Using the "random" feature is the simplest way to arrange who works with whom in breakouts. Just remember to click "re-create groups" each time you do it so the pairings/groups change throughout your session. Over time, you may decide to be more intentional about assigning groups to balance partners and perspectives. If you want to move someone to a new group, click "participants" at the bottom of Zoom and a list of who is where comes up. Hover over a name and the "reassign" option pops up.

- **Rollout:** As with your brick-and-mortar classroom, it's important to plan your Rollouts after. For instance, when Ben Esser rolls out Turn and Talk over Zoom, he first outlines a simple system for which student speaks first: alphabetical order by first name. Second, he makes clear the expectation that students will paraphrase what the person before them said. This both socializes students to carefully listen to one another and provides an entry point through which they can begin to synthesize their peers' thinking with their own.

Video Clip: Ben Esser, "Misunderstanding"

https://www.wiley.com/go/newnormal

SHARED DOCUMENTS AND STUDENT SUBMISSION

While the chat and Breakout Rooms features are useful for teachers looking to assess student work in real time, sometimes comprehensive feedback loops require longer periods of assessment. This is nothing new. Nearly all teachers are familiar with systems where students hand in work for teachers to evaluate outside of class time. In a remote setting, providing materials and feedback on student work is just as important. Even when working remotely, schools still need a system for sending lesson materials and receiving student work.

The most low-tech feedback loop involves dropping off packets over the weekend, picking them up the following weekend, and then delivering feedback the week after that.

It's slow, but even slow feedback loops are better than none at all. Fortunately, most schools and students have the ability to send and receive email. In the absence of a formal platform, a dedicated email account for the class will enable students to submit work and receive feedback asynchronously. Many schools are using a formal platform like Google Classroom, with dedicated space for students to download documents and upload their work.

In fact, digital material distribution and collection has its benefits:

- **The Digital Record:** Sometimes paper can sprout legs, pull itself out of a folder, and walk away. Nearly all of us have experienced a student who can no longer find his packet, or a student who swears that she handed in an Exit Ticket that is now missing from the pile. With an email system or a digital platform like Google Classroom, an extra article or packet is only a click away, and there's a transparent record of which assignments were and were not completed.

- **Tracking Changes:** By using "Track Changes" in a document, you and the student can track the evolution of their work over time. This kind of revision can be easier to track and read than dozens of cross-outs and margin notes. Further, having a digital record means that students can go back and review their feedback from earlier assignments, hopefully cutting down on the need for you to correct students on the same error multiple times. "Go back to unit 4 where we worked on proper citation format, and make sure you incorporate that format into your current essay as well."

Tool Tips: Shared Documents and Student Submission

- We can ask students for more than just written work. Online whiteboards like GoBoard provide a digital space for writing math equations or just drawing freehand.

- Video submission sites like Flipgrid enable students to film short video of their answer, or even film a video response to another student's submission.

- Plan for technological failures. Great teachers have contingency plans. Put packets and multimedia lesson materials in a shared folder where they can always be found. Record synchronous lessons, and make them always available in the same shared folder after they are uploaded. Provide students with clear What to Do instructions for retrieving those materials, and make explicit the expectation that students are still expected to complete their work if they have platform issues or get disconnected.

SETTING UP YOUR SPACE

We've said that great teachers prepare students for success by managing the work space. Simplicity and consistency are the guiding principles. Students need the materials they need for their lesson, and everything else is a distraction. We've established that it's important to have strong systems around organizing your workspace. This also applies to the digital space. Some folks are fortunate enough to have a reliable printer and dual monitors in their home office. The rest of us might have to start getting creative when it comes to organizing our digital workspace for teaching. We also have to be thoughtful about how we should ask students to organize their digital workspace. There are a few keys to setting up your digital workspace for teaching:

- **Build off the Slides:** PowerPoint and other presentation software allow you to embed notes, images, videos — just about anything that you would normally use as a lesson resource in your classroom. Start there. This allows you to copy and paste slides into future lessons so you can maximize format consistency and directions.

- **Avoid Switching:** Using some programs, like Zoom, it's inconvenient to swap which screen you're sharing. That's a good thing. It's a reminder that your lesson design may be too complex. Keep it simple. While there are times when you'll want to guide students through a unique format, try to minimize these occasions. Tech problems happen, and it's hard to get the class back once you've lost them.

- **Practical is better than fancy:** Embedding a timer into PowerPoint is a surprisingly complex task. As a brilliant, low-tech workaround, we were delighted to see some teachers simply hold up a timer to their web camera. Conversely, we've seen tech savvy teachers get carried away with elaborate transition animations that ultimately slowed down their lesson. As a general rule, it's best to spend your time developing content and giving feedback to students. Deprioritize tech that is more spectacle than substance.

Tool Tips: Setting Up Your Space

- **Tiny Screens:** Many students may be using their phone to watch the Zoom call. As much as possible, keep the font and images large, and don't assume that students can see the screen when they're using the chat.

- **Use Paper for Notes:** Unless you're dropping off packets at their home, assume that students do not have printed materials. Instead, students should try to take notes by hand and use their computer to view the lesson. It can be tough for students to fill in an online document while they're watching your Zoom lesson.

- **Avoid Swapping:** Avoid asking students to regularly switch applications in a synchronous class. Distractions are just a click away, and having a policy of not swapping tabs is a good way of removing the temptation to check on social media notifications. Obviously, students can still use Google Docs, but that should happen during designated periods of independent or asynchronous work; try not to ask students to fill out a document if you simultaneously want them to be learning from your PowerPoint slide.

SCREEN SHARING

As you've read throughout, Cold Call can be an exceptionally powerful tool for fostering learning and accountability. Slow to embrace classroom technology, we finally conceded that the document camera is worth its weight in gold. We saw so many teachers using the doc cam in brilliant ways that we were forced to recognize a new technique, Show Call.

In the switch from face-to-face to online classrooms, perhaps no technique translates more seamlessly than Show Call. "Screen sharing" is the online equivalent of putting a student's work up on the document camera. Without belaboring the virtues of Show Call here, let's jump into some of the ways we might Share Screen in a great lesson.

- **Bright Spots and Common Errors:** Just like a document camera Show Call, a teacher can ask students to share their screen (or select a submitted document and share their own) to highlight an exemplar process or common error.

- **Collectively Worked Example:** A teacher can also Share Screen on a word document to work with the class to form a key definition. Group revision is easier to track when the teacher is sharing her screen and Tracking Changes in real time.

- **Narrate the Positive:** Asynchronous lessons can put a strain on the relationship between teachers and their students. Using student work samples from yesterday's Exit Ticket is a great way of Dissolving the Screen and establishing the normalcy of submitting quality work.

Tool Tips: Screen Sharing

- Disable Screen Sharing until you're ready: Until you build a strong culture, students may not be able to resist the temptation to "accidentally" share something silly or inappropriate to the whole class. By default, students should not be able to share their screen. Only enable student screen sharing right before asking a student to share her work.

- Share your screen, not the application: Zoom is designed to allow you to share a specific application (like PowerPoint) with students instead of exactly what is showing on your screen. For new users, making use of this feature is more trouble than it's worth. Just share your "screen" in the upper left, and you'll be sure that whatever you see on your computer monitor is what your students are seeing as well.

- Zoom has a basic whiteboard: If you want to re-create a physics diagram or a math equation, you can use Share Screen to bring up a whiteboard. However, the tools are very basic. Unless you have a touchpad and a stylus (or a knack for this for some reason), you're likely better off using a dedicated whiteboard program that is preprogrammed with a scientific calculator and a list of common equations (e.g., GoBoard).

CLASSROOM TECH: IN REVIEW

Simplicity is key. Any solution — high tech or low — that makes the job of teaching easier and more effective is a good solution.

- **Recording Yourself:** Recording lessons from home has its challenges. Where you choose to record, against what background, and what lighting and background noise can all affect a student's learning experience. Take the time to do it right.

- **Chat:** Chat is a great way to help you maximize time, by checking in on a class all at once, or allowing you the space to review submissions later. While this shouldn't be the *only* Means of Participation, it has some clear benefits. Take advantage of them.

- **Breakout Rooms:** Use Breakout Rooms to bring some of the small-group discussion of the physical classroom to the remote setting. They're also a great way to Check for Understanding.

- **Shared Documents and Student Submission:** Sometimes comprehensive feedback loops require longer periods of assessment than the seconds it takes to write a chat. Distributing and collecting materials digitally has a number of key benefits and can save you a lot of time and effort over analog cousins.

- **Setting Up Your Space:** Setting up your digital space is as important as your workstation — for student understanding, perhaps even more so. Simplicity and consistency should guide your decisions here. Avoid tools that are more flash than substance.

- **Screen Sharing:** Screen sharing can be a great way to get techniques like Show Call into the virtual classroom. It also makes highlighting bright spots and common errors easier, makes it possible to collectively work through examples, and helps to Dissolve the Screen.

Coda: Planning for the Future

Erica Woolway, Emily Badillo, and Doug Lemov

In some ways, it's odd for us end to this book speculating about "what the future holds." One of the few things we are certain about for school in the coming years is its level of uncertainty, which will almost certainly be historic. The most honest answer to almost any question about the future is this: no one knows. And yet, schools must plan and design and implement (and hire and train and create budgets) in such a climate. Nervous laughter might be forgivable if it weren't so deadly serious. Young people are relying on us. We have to prepare, whether or not it's plausible to know what we're planning for.

Will we all be back in classrooms with our students, walking down familiar hallways? If so, how often, for how long, and under what conditions? Schools may start the year under one model, only to have things suddenly change. We start the year at home, but soon come back. We may come back, but then we're out again. This could go on for a month, a year, or even a decade.

This means that we need alignment between how we teach remotely and how we teach in person. This was among the very first things we noticed on that first morning—all of us on our laptops watching Rachel Shin on her laptop, talking to kids who would watch her later on theirs. She instantly evoked echoes of the classroom they used to share. Same phrases, similar routines. She stands up and walks to a paper taped to her window, just as if it was the whiteboard in her classroom. "Just like we always do," she says at one point. That's a phrase we heard time and again from the teachers who spoke to us most. They regularly evoked the connected social setting they have shared with their students. This stressed continuity and familiarity and calm. It said, "You know how to do this. We are still together. I see you."

For that to happen, reliably and consistently, will take some planning. Procedures and routines will have to be firmly established to translate between settings. And ideally, they'd be deliberately designed with language that bridges both worlds. We're mostly for low-tech in actual classrooms, but there's a good argument to be made for using Google Classroom or some other platform to receive student papers if you aren't already. If everyone starts turning things in remotely, that process is already in place. We did observe that schools who were already relying on a platform like Google Classroom prior to transitioning to online learning had a much gentler learning curve. Kids and families were familiar with the drill.

Another aspect of planning to think about is materials. There is a good chance we'll be moving back and forth between online and in-person settings. When we suddenly closed up shop in March and sent students home, some were (understandably) sent home empty handed. In other cases, advance planning meant a box of crayons and packets for two weeks. We've often found ourselves watching video of teachers teaching remotely with so little time to prepare and thinking: what if? What if they'd known and could have gotten every student a copy of the novel? What if they'd known and every student had a whiteboard they could use to Check for Understanding: "Ok, everyone, draw a diagram showing the water cycle and hold it up to your screen so I can see." The second time around, we can be ready for those things. We're imagining a little box for each student—a little Go Bag, with whiteboards, waiting metaphorically by the door, for use when the news comes that we're out for the next few weeks. And of course, planning for device loaning—ensuring all students have access to a device; perhaps ensuring that the device is optimized to support student learning and even restrict distractions—would be a critical piece. Same with solutions to internet access. This time around, we were caught off guard by students not having regular access to the internet. Next time, we can't be.

Another possibility is that we could return to classrooms, but the "we" might not be everybody. Some parents may choose not to send their children back. One district we know is planning for the potential for up to 25% of students to elect not to come back when school reopens (and for some percentage of those students not to have internet access). There'll be home packets and a parallel system. Again, the procedures and routines—How do we turn in papers? Where do I find my assignments?—will be doubly important. So will things like office hours. One of the ways we've tried but failed to be consistently intentional about our language is in referring to what we do as remote teaching versus online teaching. Remote is a broader category. It includes teaching online but also other tools you might use when you're far from students: emails and texts and phone calls (imagine that!). The occasional socially distanced face-to-face meeting. These are especially important tools for office hours—the individualized antidote to a mode of delivery that grows more and more scaled.

Yet another consideration for the future may be looking carefully at the school calendar. Some districts and states examined opening earlier not only to make up for lost learning gains from the spring, but also in anticipation of a possible "second wave" coming in the fall. Schools will want to consider what their remote model will look like over the summer, especially when we are all feeling the urgency around any additional learning loss for our kids—and as every month of learning lost may have an exponential impact.

And there are more questions, of course. It's unlikely that school will look the same across countries or states or even within a single district or network. We could conceivably come and go through the year with rolling levels of pandemic warnings. Students may spend half of the week in the school building and half the week doing remote instruction. Schools and districts might have little warning before a sudden shift to online learning for all students, much like the first wave of closures.

However, there are some breadcrumbs to follow in the forest of uncertainty. Beyond making sure our online and brick-and-mortar systems align, we'll also have to think seriously about building connections—before and during remote instruction. One of the most profound lessons from this year has been the realization that, hard as it was, remote learning was based on the relationships and habits we built over six months together in the classroom. Will we have that in the future? If we get it, we must not squander it. But sometimes, the harder we try for something, the less of it we accomplish. Relationships are built first and foremost through effective teaching. The goal is not that they love us—that's catnip. The goal is that they love learning by doing it with us.

ON EQUITY

As Emily Oster's discussion of John Friedman's research reminds us, we're going to come back not just to a more complex, challenging, and uncertain environment in which to teach, but also to students who are farther behind and likely with large learning gaps. Further, these gaps are likely to be distributed inequitably. Some students will have suffered more from the lack of traditional schooling. This implies at least two things about the allocation of school resources. One is that more resources will likely be required in the area of assessment. If we know that online learning is, for now, less effective, we have to use assessment more intentionally and effectively to understand the gaps. Fortunately, we can begin assessing now, as testing can be done remotely with some success. In the ideal, we'd know a lot about where our students stood, individually and as a whole, the day the buses pulled up at the school doors again.

It's also probable that we'll require different assessments in many cases. Math is more reliably assessed by our current tests. Many reading assessments, we believe, erroneously presume that reading is a set of transferrable skills—if you can draw an inference from one passage, you can draw one from all passages—and test accordingly. But reading is more likely a combination of foundational skills—fluency with varying level or complex text and syntax—and background knowledge, of which vocabulary might be the most important. If we want to know where students are in reading more reliably in the face of an urgent crisis, we'll have to shift the types of assessments we use. And of course, there's the issue that other subjects like science and history and the arts don't have standardized assessment in many cases, which puts us at risk of giving them less attention—what gets measured is what gets done, they say. We think this would be a grave mistake.

A second issue in the allocation of resources is human resources. If we know some students are especially poorly served by remote learning and if spaces in school are scarce (there are 16 seats instead of 32 in a classroom, say), could we offer some of those seats or some of the opportunities for drop-in, socially distanced, face-to-face interactions according to need? We will almost assuredly have to, as some districts we know have already begun contemplating. Who comes back first after a wave of pandemic may be who needs to be back first. This is another reason why remote assessment may be so critical.

STAFFING MODELS

Teaching is, for the most part, an individual sport—we obviously wish it was different, but it often boils down to a teacher and her classroom and you're on your own. Online learning may cause some restructuring. As schools reinvent what learning looks like, the role and responsibilities of the individual teacher must shift considerably. We have the opportunity to leverage and build the learning and leading capacities of teaching teams in an unusual way right now, and so we thought it might be helpful to explore a few possible staffing models and their potential impact.

Remote instruction liberates us to be really creative in our staffing models. As you work to land on a solution that maximizes the talent of your community of teachers to serve the needs of your students, keep the following suggestions in mind:

- **Teaching Partnerships:** Given that we no longer need to worry about how many students fit in one classroom (though how many you can see simultaneously on a screen is important), teachers can combine talents in a variety of ways. Two teachers could partner up, and one could provide all asynchronous instruction while the other facilitates live learning. In synchronous models, it may be particularly helpful to have one teacher who facilitates discussion and plans for content delivery and another who manages the chat and determines data trends from looking at student work, both during and after class.

- **Support Staff and Assistant Teachers**: There's a wide variety of options for how support staff or specialists like ESL or special education teachers can support struggling students or those who need additional resources. We like one model where the small group of students watches the asynchronous model together with the skills teacher, so that he or she is then able to insert the scaffolding and supports directly into the asynchronous lesson. Further, support staff may provide off-computer support through frequent telephone check-ins or quick checks on completed work via text, giving the student both encouragement and perhaps also feedback closer to the point of error.

LESSONS FROM SPRING

We're not likely to forget the spring of 2020 anytime soon, the school year in which all of us, with varying levels of experience, interest, and tech savvy, entered into a huge experiment in remote learning (and frankly, a lot of other things, too). Though it may have felt (and certainly felt to us) like we were all just scrambling to keep our heads above water, these chaotic months have taught us a few important lessons about teaching and learning online.

First, remote instruction opens up tremendous possibility for coaching and teacher growth. Asynchronous learning gives teachers the ability to rerecord. In one scenario, a veteran teacher might work with two or three less-experienced teachers to guide them through the feedback loop of planning, practicing, recording, and then rerecording their asynchronous lessons. More novice teachers could also grow by supporting the strongest teachers at a school on their synchronous lessons. Novice teachers could be given an observation task and also a responsibility. For example, "Note how Ms. Awesome varies her Means of Participation and checks in with these individual students during each independent work task." Eventually these novice teachers, if assigned to work in partners with stronger veterans, may take over small portions of synchronous learning and eventually the whole class, with their coach taking the role of support and feedback.

In our study of video, we've also noticed that some of our favorite techniques (particularly Economy of Language, clear What to Do directions, and Means of Participation) become even more essential online. Coaching in these areas could translate into greater success in future brick-and-mortar teaching. A teacher who spends time honing his Economy of Language in online instruction may be better able to step back into the classroom and continue to utilize those skills. We've also seen that, through technology, there are things teachers are able to do even better online than in person. For instance,

Show Calling and Cold Calling often happen seamlessly online. As teachers become more comfortable with these techniques in their remote classrooms, they may continue to use them fluidly throughout an unpredictable school year.

In our own work of teacher training, we realized that there are major implications for Professional Development (PD) opportunities. We're learning that our Train the Trainer (TTT) workshops can be effective and reach people digitally, particularly those who may not have been able to travel. In fact, in the future we are likely to add a remote TTT option to our PD offerings. What used to require people to spend both time and money to travel to a hotel (often windowless) conference room now can be joined with a simple click from across a variety of time zones. We transformed our two-day PD model to now include five 90-minute synchronous sessions complemented by asynchronous tasks, including video analysis, prereading, and practice that is recorded and sent to our team using Flipgrid. This also has allowed us to implicitly model a remote learning model for adults — one that can be adapted and applied to kids and teachers alike. For coaches and school leaders, designing and leading remote professional development for their teachers may help them gain some firsthand experience, helping develop their own capacity and allowing them to model techniques for online instruction.

Finally, leveraging existing culture and relationships has been a success of the spring. A challenge of the fall will be what to do without those prior connections. Schools may want to consider having their teachers "loop" with their students to the extent possible. If this isn't possible, partnerships and communications between teachers across the grades will make students feel more supported. This might mean having the previous year's teacher FaceTime students in the following year and allude to conversations they've had about the student. ("Ms. Watson said that you were really good at number story problems last year—can't wait to see how well you do on them this year!") For teachers who are starting the school year remotely, with students who are new to the school, the challenge is greater, but not insurmountable. Clear, consistent Systems and Routines, fostering a warm classroom culture of accountability and support, and showing students through your attention to their ideas that you care about their learning can help students feel safe, successful, and known—even if you're never in the same room together.

SILVER LININGS

We mentioned in the introduction that there would be silver linings (but no TED Talk). Some of those have begun to emerge, though more by far will emerge in time.

One benefit to our enhanced understanding of—and more universal skill with—remote learning is an increased capacity to support students when they are not in the room with us. For example, students who are at home doing homework, who are out sick, or are missing from school for whatever reason may now have resources and tools of support from teachers that we hadn't developed in prior school years.

Another potential silver lining is how much instruction you have online: all those videos of your staff explaining concepts in short, asynchronous lessons. They're evergreen, most of them. Could you use naming protocols to make it obvious to students and parents what they cover and post them somewhere so any student any time can go back and brush up on something they missed? Could you assign or suggest periodic reviews during longer breaks to reduce learning loss?

Having broken the barriers of time and place, we have also potentially opened the door to better and greater use of one of teaching's scarcest commodities: specific expertise. One of the biggest challenges for many schools is finding teachers with technical knowledge in things like physics and chemistry and higher math. Just imagine running a district of 15 high schools in a relatively large city and therefore needing 15 (or perhaps 30 or 45) people who have the knowledge and desire to teach high school calculus or physics. Could the familiarity of the "system" (meaning all of us) with online learning formats and hybrids allow one physics teacher to do one or two highly technical classes for large groups, or asynchronously across multiple schools with science teachers of more general knowledge—but high teaching skills—who teach the follow lessons on site? Perhaps.

The scarcity of time and attention online also has the potential to be a silver lining, because it forces us to pay attention to the demands of working memory. It makes us more aware of attention. Utilizing Pause Points to consolidate memory, incorporating frequent retrieval practice, being aware of cognitive load, and using strong Systems and Routines to support all of these components: remote learning puts these concerns front and center, but they are potentially high-leverage changes we can make to our in-person classrooms as well.

MAINTAINING WHAT MATTERS

The biggest lesson we've learned from this unprecedented spring may have been one we already knew, one we learn all over again each school year. The relationships between teachers and students, the commitment of teachers to improving their craft, to reaching their students, to ensuring their students grow—these are still what matters most. The institution of schooling as we know it may be changed forever, or only temporarily disrupted. Who's to say what the autumn of 2021 will look like, let alone the autumn of 2025. But we know that, no matter the model, no matter the technology or the location or the new guidelines, when teachers plan carefully, build strong Systems and Routines, and respond to their students' understanding, students will learn and develop, feel seen and valued, and continue their educations, whether they're seated in our classrooms or on their couches. Teachers first and foremost build a culture around their students, one that shapes their understanding of content, but also their perception of the world and their place in it. That work is harder to do when we are remote some or all of the time, but it's still doable, especially if one of our primary takeaways from our time in the New Normal is to realize anew, and with renewed emphasis, the critical value of the culture we build.

Glossary of Teach Like a Champion (TLAC) Techniques

Acknowledge versus Praise Acknowledging student contributions without overpraising routine behaviors. Helps keep actual praise for exemplary work meaningful.

Brighten Lines Transitions that serve to emphasize the boundaries between activities or sections of a lesson. Helps with Pacing, and to give lessons a more dynamic feel for teachers and students.

Check for Understanding Tools used to gather and assess real-time data on student understanding of a particular concept, topic, or lesson, *before the end of the lesson*. Particularly important in remote settings.

Cold Call Calling on a student regardless of whether they have raised their hand or otherwise volunteered. Good tool for ensuring accountability, preparedness, and engagement.

Collectively Worked Example When students and teachers build a model response to a problem or questions together. Fosters teamwork, humility, and group understanding.

Control the Game System for focusing students' oral reading on a shared passage. Helps make in-class reading more productive, accountable, and efficient.

Culture of Error Creating (virtual) classrooms where students are comfortable revealing mistakes and value them as learning opportunities.

Do Now A short activity students complete immediately, often at the beginning of a lesson. Signals that we are here to learn and helps kickstart the lesson.

Economy of Language Habit of avoiding extraneous language in communicating. Helps ensure directions are clear and lessons are more efficient.

Everybody Writes Giving students a chance to reflect in writing before a discussion. Helps students prepare for rigorous discussion, and lowers cognitive load by removing the need to commit written notes to memory.

Means of Participation Any of the many ways teachers can engineer active student participation into lessons.

Narrate the Positive Act of naming and acknowledging students who are meeting and exceeding expectations.

Pacing The practice of making rigorous work on a given topic feel energetic and forward-moving.

Ratio Strategy for shifting the cognitive work of a lesson onto students. Important for fostering independent thinking.

Retrieval Practice Any exercise where students must recall and reapply previously mastered content.

Rollout An explanation, for students, of the *what-and-the-why* for any classroom approach you are using, particularly new ones.

Show Call A type of Cold Call that involves taking students' written work and displaying it to the class.

Show Me Process by which students show their teacher objective data of their work (via hand signals or slates or some other online answering mechanism) in unison so that teachers can quickly assess it.

Stop and Jot Pausing a lesson briefly for students to "jot" down initial thought and ideas in response to a prompt.

Turn and Talk Tool by which teachers facilitate small-group discussions. In physical classroom, literally often "turning and talking" to partners. Online, may occur in chats or Breakout Rooms.

Wait Time Deliberately waiting a few extra seconds after asking a question before calling on someone to answer it. Allows more students (not just the fastest) a chance to participate.

What to Do Exceedingly clear directions for any classroom task (remote or in-person).

Notes

INTRODUCTION

1. Emily Oster, "COVID-19, Learning Loss and Inequality," *Parent Data*, June 15, 2020, https://emilyoster.substack.com/p/covid-19-learning-loss-and-inequality.

CHAPTER 3

1. Daisy Christodoulou, *Teachers vs Tech? The Case for an Ed Tech Revolution* (Oxford, UK: Oxford University Press, 2020), p. 139.

2. Ibid, p. 140.

3. Ibid.

4. Maryanne Wolf, *Reader, Come Home: The Reading Brain in a Digital World* (New York: Harper, 2018).

5. Manyu Jiang, "The Reason Zoom Calls Drain Your Energy," BBC, April 22, 2020, https://www.bbc.com/worklife/article/20200421-why-zoom-video-chats-are-so-exhausting.

A Lesson Template and the Concept of the Semisynchronous Task

This appendix represents insights our team had after the deadline for the manuscript of this book. Happily we were able to include it. Please be aware that further updates and insights, along with video examples, can be found at our blog: https://teachlikeachampion.com/blog/

Darryl Williams leads team TLAC's partnership work, where we work directly with schools to help them achieve their vision of high-quality equitable instruction in every classroom. Working directly with schools as they began to put together plans for the 2020-21 school year, he found himself side by side with schools making hard decisions about emerging challenges.

He put together a draft "framework" for what the structure of online lessons could look like across a school. Schools need some consistency. Having a model for what a lesson should generally look like helps teachers plan. And not just classroom teachers but Special Educators and other personnel who provide services to students. How could consistency and flexibility be combined?

Darryl put together a model that drew on the fact that the biggest challenge of both synchronous and asynchronous instruction is, arguably, the same thing: fatigue, tuning out, exhaustion. We know students need face-to-face interactions. But even for adults, several hours of Zoom time can be brutal. But asynchronous learning can also be exhausting and isolating. Being on the receiving end of constant string of emailed assignments or impersonal-seeming asynchronous videos can also wear a student out.

The beauty of Darryl's framework is how it balances the two types of instruction to make online learning both productive and sustainable.

First here's an overview of what he proposed, adapted to a hypothetical 60 minute class that meets each Monday, Wednesday and Friday at 9:00.

I should note that the idea is that this model is not a mandate .... it would be adapted differently by each school and probably routinely adapted by teachers. But it sets a general structure that's productive and sustainable and brings some necessary predictability and consistency to what teaching could look like.

In the **Lesson Opening**, students and teacher are present synchronously. We'd want a teacher to seek constant interaction so students feel connected, included and accountable: quick writes and chats and Cold Calls and maybe a quick breakout in pairs.

	Lesson Opening (15 min) 9:00-9:15am	Partner & Independent Work (15 min) 9:15-9:30am	Lesson Closing (15 min) 9:30-9:45am	Flex Time (15 min) 9:45-10:00am
Essential Elements	Welcome: Warm & engaging but brief. Engage student actively w/in First 3! Teach new content or explore more about previous topic. Discuss a model problem (high levels of student interaction). Shared reading.	Students complete work independently or w partners. Student may be semi-asynchronous (i.e. still with cameras on) or, later, fully asynchronous. Students view asynchronous lesson video. Independent reading.	Back to fully synchronous. Review and revise independent work. Study misconceptions. Lesson summary (i.e. Stamp.) Set expectations for homework completion and submission Shared reading or re-reading.	Individual or small-group check-ins or reteach. Homework started and/or submitted- Shared or independent reading. Retrieval Practice
Key Visual	Start "face visible." Then, Orientation Screen: Materials needed; overview of lesson.	Overview Screen: Directions for independent task, ideally remains visible throughout	As much face visible as possible.	Closing Screen: Clear explanation of what is due when & how to submit.

The lesson should start with students seeing a smiling face and being asked to do something active–respond to a question in the Zoom chat, say–within the first three minutes. There should be an 'orientation screen' near to the beginning so students know what materials they need to participate and sense that things are planned and time is important.

The focus is on direct teaching here. Teach new content. Read a passage from the novel. Work a model problem. Bit with lots of interaction. Perhaps for 10-15 minutes.

After ten or fifteen minutes of everyone together, connected and accountable, maybe it's time for some **Independent Work**. In most cases it would '**semi-synchronous**,' as Knikki and Eric do in these two videos [video]: cameras on so you can support and check in with students as Eric does brilliantly, making his students feel seen and heard even though they're reading independently. And notice that the directions are up on his screen the whole time in case students forget. Or notice how Knikki questions so carefully to make sure students understand the task. They work independently but they also work hard. They can probably guess that they're going to get cold called afterwards.

After a bit of independent work maybe it's time to come back to a synchronous setting for the **Lesson Closing** in which the teacher is focused on checking for understanding, ad reviewing the independent work, making sure students were productive and successful on their own. That might look at bit like this clip of Ben Esser's lesson, which again is highly interactive ... there's a great writing prompt that everyone completes. There are loving Cold Calls. There are breakout rooms (and Ben drops in to one to see how it's going) etc.

At the end the lesson shifts again to what we call **Flex Time** ... students get some (or all!) of their homework done.

There's time for you to check in with individuals or small groups who need more support. It's a great time to offer targeted support for students who require accommodations or special education services... and the fact that the time is relatively predictable makes it easier for them to provide support. Kids might even get to do a little reading. But you'd also want to be really clear: what work is due when? Submitted how?

Like the **Independent Work** block Flex Time could be semi-synchronous. Or perhaps fully asynchronous with some or all students signing off.

One of the big takeaways from the model is the structure of those independent blocks and the realization that they aren't really fully asynchronous. Here are some of the elements in common that make both Eric and Knikki's independent tasks semi-synchronous:

- Both Eric and Knikki give students a specific amount of time to work on a task for. Both teachers ask students if they need more time. Attending to time is critical. Too short and the task doesn't get completed. Too long and student attention fades.

- Both then bring students back from the independent work and review immediately.

- The tasks require students to use paper and pencil (or to read a book) in other words they are not looking at a screen. This is hugely important. Massive doses of screen time are hard on the brain. These moments offer refreshing breaks.

- Both teachers use the transition out of synchronous teaching to ensure that students understand the task. Eric posts the directions on his screen so students can refer to it throughout while they work. Knikki very deliberately checks for understanding of the task–what are we doing? where are we writing? She asks via Cold Call. It is the only time she uses English.

- They remind us that students (no, people) are inherently more distracted and distractible online. "Learning to concentrate is an essential but ever more difficult challenge in a culture where distraction is omnipresent," writes Maryanne Wolf. Both teachers here are socializing sustained periods of work that reinforce strong attention and they are able to hold students lovingly accountable for maintaining that attention.